2024-2025 EDITION

10th GRADE READY

EXPERT ADVICE TO HELP PARENTS NAVIGATE THE YEAR AHEAD

EDITED BY
TIMOTHY M. DOVE

A READY GUIDE

PARENT READY!

PARENT READY

2024 Edition
Copyright © 2024 Parent Ready, Inc.

Parent Ready supports the right to free expression and the value of copyright. The purpose of copyright is to encourage the creation of works that enrich our culture.

All rights reserved. No part of this book may be reprinted or reproduced in any form or by any electronic, mechanical, or other means, now known or hereafter invented, including photocopying, recording, and information storage and retrieval, without the prior written permission of the publisher, except in the case of brief quotations embodied in critical articles and reviews.

Published by Parent Ready, Inc.
8 East Windsor Avenue
Alexandria, Virginia 22301
https://parentready.com

Parent Ready and design are trademarks of Parent Ready, Inc.

The publisher is not responsible for websites (or their contents) that are not owned by the publisher.

ISBN: 979-8-9893392-9-7 (paperback)
ISBN: 979-8-9893392-8-0 (e-book)

Bulk purchases: Quantity discounts are available. Please make inquiries via https://gradeready.guide.

Table of Contents

Contributors vii

Foreword xv
    David A. Echols, JD, MEd-EDL

Introduction xix
    Timothy M. Dove

Chapter 1: How Is 10th Grade Different from 9th Grade? 1
    How to support your teen during this transitional year
    Mandy Manning

Chapter 2: How Is a 10th Grader Different from a 9th Grader? 9
    What to expect from your high school sophomore
    Stacey Donaldson, PhD, NBCT

Chapter 3: A Deeper Dive into Course Selection 15
    What to ask your teen before they choose classes
    David Bosso

Chapter 4: Inclusion and Belonging. 23
    How your teen finds their people
    Al Rabanera

Chapter 5: The Dos and Don'ts of Success 31
    How to support your teen in the classroom
    Chris Grouzes

Chapter 6: Failing Forward 41
    How to support your teen in handling academic setbacks
    Heidi Crumrine

Chapter 7: Different Learning Styles and Accommodations 53
   What to do if you notice your teen working hard but struggling
   La-Shanda West, EdS

Chapter 8: Challenging Student-Teacher Relationships 65
   How to know when to step in and help your teen
   Renee Jones

Chapter 9: Constructive Parent-School Relationships. 77
   How to keep it positive
   Brian Skinner

Chapter 10: Online Connections 87
   How technology affects your student in and out of school
   Charlie McAdoo II, EdD

Chapter 11: Finding Passions In and Out of School. 97
   How to support your student's interests
   Jada Reeves

Chapter 12: Finding Passion in Sport 107
   How to support your high school athlete
   Sara Skretta, EdD, PHR

Chapter 13: Finding Passion in the Arts 117
   How to support your high school artist
   Sheena Graham

Chapter 14: Is My Student Ready for 11th Grade?. 125
   Advice from an 11th grade teacher (and parent also in the
      trenches of the high school years)
   Amybeth Taylor

This series of books is dedicated to all those who contribute to the education and support of young people. I was lucky enough to be a classroom teacher for 32 years. I owe a lot of my effectiveness to those who worked with me and those who taught me so much over the years, especially two master educators, Jenelle and Mark Dove, my parents. We all have teachers we think back on who made important contributions to our formal and informal education. Our parents and classroom teachers encourage, question, teach, and celebrate our students. I want to thank my colleagues who participated in this project. We can always learn from one another, and having many voices in this conversation is so helpful. Thank you to all the educators who are still engaged in this sacred trust.

—Timothy M. Dove

Contributors

Editor

Timothy M. Dove, an educator for 42 years, was the Ohio State Teacher of the Year in 2011 and 2012. Dove was a middle school teacher for 32 years and helped develop a new Global Scholars Program. He taught high schoolers for three years, was an adjunct professor at The Ohio State University for 20 years, and for the past decade has worked with national and state education agencies supporting educators and students in a variety of ways. He has been a consultant with Battelle for Kids in Hong Kong, Learning Forward, the Council of Chief State School Officers (CCSSO), and the Collaboration for Effective Educator Development, Accountability, and Reform (CEEDAR) Center.

Contributors

David Bosso is the 2012 Connecticut Teacher of the Year, the 2012 National Secondary Social Studies Teacher of the Year, and a 2019 inductee into the National Teachers Hall of Fame. Over the course of his career, he has traveled to Africa, Asia, the Middle East, and Europe to work with international peers and to enrich students' understanding of global issues. He currently serves as the president of the Connecticut Teacher of the Year Council and is a past president of the Connecticut Council for the Social Studies. Bosso holds master's degrees from the University of Hartford and Central Connecticut State University and a doctorate from American International College.

Heidi Crumrine is an English teacher and literacy coach at Concord High School in Concord, New Hampshire, where she has taught since 2004 after teaching three years in the New York City Public School system. The 2018 New Hampshire Teacher of the Year, Crumrine's writing has been published in the *Concord Monitor, Education Post, New Hampshire Bulletin, Granite Post,* and in blogs for Teaching4Tomorrow, Heinemann, and the National Network of State Teachers of the Year. Her students' work has been featured on New Hampshire Public Radio and the We Are America Project. She is also the author of *50 Strategies for Motivating Reluctant Readers.* Crumrine serves on the board of Reaching Higher NH.

David Echols, JD, MEd-EDL, is the behavior interventionist for the Lamar County School District in Hattiesburg, Mississippi. He has a passion for mentoring students who have been underprivileged and lacked positive guidance and role models in their lives. He has served as school testing coordinator, teacher coordinator, and principal in the same district. Echols graduated with a Bachelor of Science degree from Alabama State University in 1995. He graduated with a Doctor of Jurisprudence from the University of Mississippi law school in 2006 and practiced law for 10 years at the law firm of Bryan Nelson, P.A. in Hattiesburg. He also received a master's in educational leadership from William Carey University.

Dr. Stacey Donaldson is a 25-year educator and the 2010 National State Teacher of the Year from Mississippi. An assistant professor at Belhaven University, Donaldson directs the TESOL program. Before joining Belhaven, Donaldson organized Learn Elation, LLC, supporting English language arts teachers, National Board candidates, and high school students. Donaldson is board-certified in career and technical education and has been involved in various aspects of mentoring and support for teachers pursuing certification for the past 18 years. She earned a PhD in education from Walden University in 2016 and published her award-winning memoir, *Psalm 23: Wonders* *of God's Love,* in 2008. She's married to Johnny Donaldson, and they have two daughters, Camaryn and Cailyn.

Sheena Graham began teaching in 1983 and offered workshops on music literacy and connecting parents, students, and teachers. Her recording and writing experience is extensive. Graham's original works have been performed locally in her community, at the Kennedy Center in Washington, D.C., and twice at the White House. Her passion for education and the arts was recognized with the Beard Excellence in Teaching Award, the Phi Delta Kappa Educator's Golden Apple award, and Teacher of the Year Awards from the NANBP, NAACP, and Bridgeport. She is Connecticut's 2019 Teacher of the Year and is the author of *Hesitations,* a book of poetry and reflections.

Chris Grouzes teaches English, communication studies, and theatre at Penncrest High School in Media, Pennsylvania. During his 17-year career, he has worked with students in grades 6–12 as their teacher, director, speaking coach, and improv coach. Grouzes is also founder and president of Advanced Tutoring Network, a group that specializes in executive function coaching and celebrates and advocates for neurodiversity. A proud ADHDer himself, Grouzes promotes an atmosphere for his students, colleagues, and clients that encourages rigor and creativity combined with sincere discussion and cultural perspectives. Self-advocacy, acceptance, and laughter are at the core of his personal philosophy and teaching method.

Renee Jones teaches English at Lincoln High School in Lincoln, Nebraska. She emphasizes building relationships between all members of her classroom to increase student advancement. Jones received her Bachelor of Arts degree in criminology and criminal justice from the University of Nebraska Omaha. She obtained her master's in educational leadership in 2020 from Doane University. Jones was the 2019 recipient of the Lincoln Public Schools Inspire Award. She is the 2023 Nebraska Teacher of the Year. Jones is working to build classroom connection strategies and amplify the voice of teachers. She can be followed on X (formerly Twitter) at @ReneeJonesTeach.

Mandy Manning was the 2018 Washington State and National Teacher of the Year. After 21 years as a classroom teacher, she became digital content specialist for the Washington Education Association, advocating for educators, public schools, and students. Previously, Manning was the first teacher for newly arrived refugee and immigrant students at the Newcomer Center at Ferris High School in Spokane, Washington. She serves on several education-related boards, including the Spectrum Center Board, serving the LGBTQ+ community in Spokane. Manning is co-author of *Creating a Sense of Belonging for Immigrant and Refugee Students: Strategies for K–12 Educators*. Her book, *50 Strategies for Teaching Multilingual Learners*, is forthcoming from Teacher Created Materials in spring 2024.

Charlie E. McAdoo II, EdD, is a veteran career and technical educator. He has taught middle school, high school, and on the postsecondary level. Currently, he teaches in the city schools of Decatur, Georgia. He has served in various leadership capacities, such as CTE Advisory Committee Member, FBLA Sponsor, CTE Department Chair, School Leadership Team, CTE Intern Advisor, IB Design Cycle Trainer, PBIS Committee Member, and Equity Team Chair. McAdoo was a 2019 Georgia CTAE LEAD fellow, an inaugural Association of Career and Technical Education IAED Mentor, and a 2024 Teach Plus National Policy Advisory Board Fellow. McAdoo completed his BA at Clark Atlanta University, MEd from the University of West Georgia, and has an EdD from Valdosta State University in Adult and Career Education. His professional interests include mentorship program needs assessment and curriculum development.

Al Rabanera, EdD is a high school math teacher at La Vista High School in Fullerton, California. He assisted in the development and implementation of new programs that promote the retention of current teachers and encourage new generations of students to pursue careers in teaching. Rabanera is an advocate for educators, having served on the Board of Directors for North Orange County United Teachers, California Teachers Associations – Institute for Teaching, and the Council for the Accreditation of Educator Preparation. As a result of his efforts, in 2017, Rabanera was one of five educators to receive the Horace Mann Award for Teaching Excellence and selected to participate as a Global Learning Fellow. In 2018, he was selected as a recipient of the Distinguished Alumni of the Year for the College of Education at California State University Fullerton. In 2019-20, he served as a Teach Plus California Policy Fellow and is currently a Senior National Policy Advisory Board Member. Rabanera earned his doctorate from University of Southern California. He is married to Cassandra, and they have a son, Nehemiah, and a daughter, Aurora.

Jada Reeves, 2019 West Virginia State Teacher of the Year, is an academic coach for Raleigh County Schools in southern West Virginia. Reeves earned a Bachelor of Science in elementary education K–6, a reading specialist master's degree, a National Board Certification in literacy and language for early and middle elementary school, and an administrator's certificate. Reeves is pursuing a doctorate in curriculum, instruction, and assessment through Walden University. She is an online facilitator for the eLearning for Educators program through the West Virginia Department of Education (WVDE). Reeves is the lead coordinator for the Southern WV National Board Certification cohort through the WVDE and serves as one of its facilitators for awareness in certification. She is actively involved in the WV division of the Elevating and Celebrating Effective Teaching and Teachers and is a member of the planning committee. Reeves contributes to the National Board for Professional Teaching Standards blog, *The Standard*.

Brian Skinner, 2023 Kansas Teacher of the Year, is an interrelated special education teacher, grades 9–12, for Newton Schools. He has been teaching since August 2013 and serves as Newton High School's special education department chair. Skinner has also served as the individualized education plan case manager for Project SEARCH, a one-year program that focuses on vocational skills within the community for students with significant disabilities. Skinner holds a Bachelor of Arts in history from Bethel College and a masters of teaching and learning from Friends University. He is also an active member of the National Education Association at the local, regional, and state levels.

Dr. Sara Skretta is the senior director of Accreditation, Placement & Licensure in the College of Education and Human Sciences at the University of Nebraska, Lincoln. With more than 30 years in education, she served high school students as an English teacher, coach, and assistant principal. Skretta has been a Nebraska Assistant Principal of the Year, a finalist for the NSASSP National Assistant Principal of the Year, and in state and national leadership roles related to educator preparation and educator workforce challenges. Skretta is married to an educator and is most proud of their four sons.

Amybeth Taylor, who has more than 15 years of experience in secondary English education, currently teaches 11th- and 12th-grade students in Newmarket, New Hampshire. Her journey in education began as a Teach for America corps member in Los Angeles, California. Taylor holds a master's in education from the University of New Hampshire and a graduate certificate in ESOL instruction from California State University, Dominguez Hills. Her commitment to innovative education extends beyond the classroom, evident in her advocacy work with nonprofits and experience in curriculum design. Taylor strives to create authentic learning experiences for her students, nurturing a lifelong appreciation for literature and writing.

La-Shanda West has served the Miami-Dade County Public School District for 22 years, teaching secondary social studies. Her philosophy of teaching is it takes a village to educate the whole child through care, support, and stakeholder involvement. Her leadership experience includes being the iPrep Academy Leader, Donors Choose Teacher Ambassador, and Teach Better Ambassador. West holds a master's in reading K–12 from Florida Memorial University and an educational specialist degree in educational leadership from Grand Canyon University. West's accolades include the 2022 Returned Peace Corps Volunteers of South Florida Changemaking Education Award, 2021 Veterans of Foreign Wars Teacher of the Year award, 2016 National Celebrity Educator award, 2005 Miami-Dade Council for the Social Studies Teacher of the Year, and 2002 Florida Social Studies Beginning Teacher of the Year.

Foreword

David A. Echols, JD, MEd-EDL

As an attorney who has handled my share of family law cases, an educator for almost 30 years, and a single parent of three children, I have experienced the interactions between parents and students from a few different perspectives. Some of those interactions were wonderful, and others were not so wonderful. I have also seen the struggles and confusion parents have faced when dealing with their adolescent children. I have personally faced some of those struggles when my son and daughter reached their 15th birthdays, and I am sure I will be greeted with some when my third child reaches that age. I know that I, along with all the other parents I have observed and spoken with, am not alone. Furthermore, I have seen many adolescents struggle adjusting to being what I call a *tweener*—you know, that age where the child is caught between still wanting to be a little boy or girl at times and wanting to be treated as an adult at others.

Your student's sophomore year can present some challenges for them[*] and for you. For many parents, it is hard to let go of their *baby*. But they are not a baby anymore—at least not in their mind. At the same time, they are not quite an adult either. Parents and caregivers are often caught between the sentiments of "You are still a child" and

---

[*] The pronoun they/them is used in its singular form throughout the book because it is the most practical and inclusive approach.

"When are you going to grow up and act your age?" This can be a trying time for both parties. Parents must understand the unique positions that their 10th graders are in. By the same token, the students must attempt to understand the unique position parents find themselves in: letting go of trying to protect their children and instead watching them fail or succeed, experience life, and learn to grow and become productive adults.

We must consider, and be continually mindful of, the importance of communication. In all my years of dealing with and observing parents and students, the most important piece I have found missing in their relationships are communication and respect. Communicating with someone is more than just talking with them. It involves *communing* with them. The word "communicate" literally means "become one with or to unite with someone." This book can aid parents in communicating better with their children by giving valuable insight into what is going on with most 15-year-olds.

Whether we want it to or not, times are changing, and students are feeling and becoming more and more isolated. Technological advancements and the learning curve of parents who need to keep up with those advancements means that the gap seems to be ever increasing between teenagers and adults. Yes, there is a gap between *us* and *them*. If you do not believe it, ask the average teenager if they feel that they are understood by adults. Ask them if they believe the average adult listens to them and takes their opinions seriously. Ask them if they feel comfortable sitting down talking with the average adult about personal problems they are facing. Once we understand some of the doubts, indecisions, and fears that our children face, we will be better prepared to converse with them and reach them on a human-to-human level and not look down on them as if they are less than because of their age.

The purpose of this book is to help build a bridge of understanding about what a student may experience and what they should expect during their sophomore year of high school. It is written to highlight some of the potential pitfalls that may be encountered and to help parents and students either maneuver through or around those pitfalls or help them recover after falling into them. It is designed to be a reference guide for parents whose teens are entering their sophomore year of high school so they can help their kids traverse through some of the challenges they may face during this phase of their lives. It is not designed to be a panacea for all things 10th grade. However, it will alleviate some of the angst and uncertainty that students and parents may face during this time of transition.

This book is chock-full of advice and suggestions from top educators from around the country, whose expertise will not only provide you with a wealth of knowledge and valuable insights on your 10th-grade journey, but will also spark conversations and personal communications between you and your child that will reestablish broken relationships and further strengthen already established ones.

Introduction

Timothy M. Dove
2011 & 2012 Ohio State Teacher of the Year

This book is for parents, family members, caregivers, siblings, mentors, and any supporters of a soon-to-be 10th grader. Think of each of these chapters as advice from a friendly teacher in your child's school.

Each contributor to *10th Grade Ready* is a current or former 10th-grade educator who has worked extensively with parents and families of students. These contributors have all been Teachers of the Year, finalists for that award, and/or recognized for their abilities in their state. They are experts in the field overall and in the particular chapters they penned.

The chapters that follow cover many of the topics that you may be thinking about as your teen enters 10th grade. Beginning with how 10th grade differs from 9th and moving through preparing them for 11th grade, this book will serve as your guide. It will describe what to expect in a variety of areas and things to look for as you navigate your teen's physical, emotional, and academic growth. This book focuses on both action items and tips on how to support your student as they start developing their independence. Some information might seem obvious, while other pieces will be eye-opening. Every family is different, and parts of the book will resonate differently with each reader. Any new information can help you plan and engage with your child.

That which you are already familiar with should assure you that you are on the right track.

Most chapters give prompts throughout their narrative or conclude with a list of conversation starters. In thinking about how to use them, consider your student's history, your relationship with them, and other family dynamics. Using open-ended questions is the best way to get information from your student. Not only will having these conversations assist you in supporting your 10th grader, but they will also open new lines of communication that can continue throughout the school year and beyond.

This book can be used in different ways. You can focus on the chapters needed, or of interest, based on timing, or you can read it straight through to get a feel for the overall landscape of sophomore year. Tenth grade may be the year in which your student hits their stride, or they may hit the sophomore slump. Either way, we hope this book helps you navigate it.

Chapter 1

HOW IS 10TH GRADE DIFFERENT FROM 9TH GRADE?

How to support your teen during this transitional year

Mandy Manning
2018 National and Washington State Teacher of the Year

Having taught students at every level of high school during my 21 years as a classroom teacher, I have witnessed that moving from 9th grade to 10th grade can be jarring for students. Tenth grade is an interesting year. The excitement and nervousness students felt as they entered high school for the first time has worn off and, while they feel more confident as high school sophomores who better understand the system and expectations in school, they may find themselves confused about who they are, where they stand, and where they are headed. Tenth grade is the year when students can feel stuck in the middle.

Their role in the school hierarchy is unclear and they face increased academic pressures, along with the demand for them to be self-directed, independent learners. Without support and guidance, 10th graders can lose their way. Confidence and adaptability are critical character traits for sophomores as they begin to develop their personal identities, experience the freedom of learning to drive, and focus more intentionally on college and career preparation and the academic rigors and social pressures that continue to increase each year.

My own children faced these challenges. Tenth grade was the year my daughter realized she had to let go of sports that no longer served her, no longer increased her confidence, and had become a distraction from her schoolwork. My son also floundered when he entered 10th grade. He had switched schools from a K–12 environment, in which he was a big fish in a small pond, to a larger high school and had to adjust to a new academic and social environment in which most students had already been there a year and had found their communities. As a teacher and their parent, I recognized that my role was not to protect them from these challenges. My role was to support them in developing the skills to cope with the challenges ahead, honoring their burgeoning independence while quietly helping them stay focused on their academic and future goals.

The Academic Difference

Students experience a jump in academic rigor between middle school and high school, and the jump between grades in high school can be significant, as well. Students are often accessing advanced coursework such as Advanced Placement (AP) classes and continuing to focus on core subject areas. They need to set academic goals that can be achieved independently. At this stage, students are expected to track due dates and be self-directed in completing assignments and projects. Students must also hone their study skills, as they are generally responsible for their own test preparation.

In 10th grade, course selection is an important consideration, as there is little time to make up for missed credits, failed classes, or gaps in their graduation plan. Students at this grade level choose their own classes, which can lead to missteps if they do not have a strong grasp of graduation requirements and the courses they need to move toward on-time graduation. Make sure they run their choices by their high school counselor. Additionally, elective options often expand for students in 10th grade, giving them the chance to take classes based on their interests and future goals. Elective choices differ depending on a student's individual pathway toward graduation and can be dependent on their college and career plans. Students need support in assessing their progress toward graduation and course requirements to make informed decisions about the classes they need. This support can be in the form of reviewing the course catalog with your child, encouraging them to meet with their counselor, and helping them review their progress toward graduation and their remaining requirements. See chapter 3 for more on course selection.

Most schools require students to complete a college and career plan. Each year they add to this plan to help them set goals and make academic and extracurricular activity decisions. At this stage in their academic career, students are getting serious about meeting their short-term goals to serve their longer-term goals based on their post-high school plan. Your teen needs your support in revisiting their plan, adjusting based on new interests or passions, and critically examining their academic pathway to ensure they are making course and extracurricular choices that serve their goals.

An additional stressor students face in 10th grade is test-taking. The PSAT (the Preliminary Scholastic Assessment Test), a practice exam for the SAT, is a requirement for applying for some colleges and universities, although many have become test-optional since the COVID pandemic. It is also the National Merit Scholarship Qualifying Test, so students who score high enough on the PSAT are eligible for National Merit Scholarships. The PSAT is a standardized test, which can cause anxiety for students, especially if they feel pressured to do well on the exam. Tenth grade is also a year in which many students are required to take state-level standardized assessments needed for graduation. Students need support in dealing with test anxiety and recognizing that these tests are not a measure of their intelligence or abilities. Here are some easy ways to help your child deal with test anxiety:

- Breathing exercises to refocus the brain
- Maintaining good posture
- Getting enough sleep
- Breaking down test instructions into smaller parts

Finally, assure your student that regardless of their performance on these tests, there are many pathways toward achieving their personal and professional goals. Many states offer multiple pathways toward graduation, such as specific coursework, completing performance-based projects, state standardized tests, taking dual-credit classes, or accessing a career-technical education pathway. Help your student learn about the pathways available in your state.

Extracurricular Considerations

By 10th grade, students are still developing their passions and choosing to continue with activities depending on whether those activities serve their interests and goals. Students are figuring out what they most enjoy and what gives them confidence. They are learning to leave behind activities they are no longer passionate about and moving on to new activities or pouring more time into those activities they love. Students need support in pursuing activities that will serve their future goals and in leaving behind sports and activities they no longer enjoy. This can be difficult for parents, especially if they deem their child to be talented in a sport or activity that their child no longer wishes to pursue. Parental support is critical in helping teens become independent, self-advocating, and learning to make productive choices for themselves, including recognizing the extracurricular activities that enrich and serve them as they move toward adulthood. See chapters 11–13 for more on extracurricular activities.

Tenth grade is a time when students are beginning to take on more responsibility through leadership roles in clubs and on sports teams. Students are running for class office, club officer positions, and taking on additional responsibilities on projects and in activities related to their extracurricular endeavors. While leadership roles are critical for character development and for learning to collaborate and work on teams, balancing these roles with academic responsibilities can prove difficult, especially if students are also taking on part-time jobs outside of school or doing community service and volunteering. Organizational skills are critical as students pursue these opportunities. Help them maintain a calendar to track their various obligations, events, and due dates to ensure they can stay afloat and on track to graduate. Students may need reminders that balance is important and gentle nudging to drop any activities that are not serving their future goals or personal interests.

Social Dynamics and the Pressures of 10th Grade

By 10th grade, social groups are more established and many students find school events, such as dances, to be more enjoyable, as they find safety within their friend groups. However, as was the case with my son, this can be difficult for students who transfer in from another school or community. Students have generally found their place within a group of peers based on their personal interests and identities (see chapter 4 for more on this). Many students are still figuring out who they are and may shift between groups if they have adjusted their extracurricular activities, joined something new, or left something else behind. These transitions are difficult, and students can feel lonely, disconnected, or unsure of where they belong. Confidence and self-esteem play a big role in whether students successfully navigate high school friendships. Students need support in navigating personal relationships, setting personal boundaries, and working through conflict. Chapters 4–8 will help parents establish this support.

Increased freedom influences social relationships in 10th grade. Students are reaching a new milestone, learning to drive, and getting their licenses, depending on when their birthday falls during the school year and the rules within their households. Driving brings a new sense of freedom and can grant access to more activities outside of school. Driving can also lead to errors in judgment and risk-taking. Teach your teens to be responsible as drivers *and* as passengers, and provide guidelines, such as how many passengers they can have in the car and where and when they can drive, to ensure they are continuing to prioritize school and meeting their goals for their futures.

How to Support Your Child

You know your child needs increasing independence balanced with your guidance to make good decisions. Here is a list of basic supports you can offer:

1. **Create a schedule.** Post a calendar that you and your child use to track all your child's obligations—academic, extracurricular, social, and familial. This will help them visualize their schedule and attempt to balance everything.

2. **Help prioritize.** Look at the calendar weekly and assess the workload. Help your child determine what needs to be a priority and whether they need to adjust their schedule to ensure they can complete everything.

3. **Help set achievable goals.** Help your child break down tasks, activities, assignments, and projects into smaller pieces so they can get them done little by little to leave time for extracurriculars and social activities.

4. **Focus on time management.** With driving and social opportunities, time management is critical in staying focused on academic responsibilities, as is critical self-reflection and learning to say "no." Help your child recognize when they have taken on too much and need to cut back.

5. **Model and encourage self-care.** Eating right and getting enough sleep are essential to high school success. Try to ensure that your child has at least one healthy meal a day and use that time to connect and check in about how they are doing socially and academically. Help your child find time to relax and encourage them to make healthy, positive choices.

Closing Advice

Tenth grade will be challenging. The newness of high school has gone away, yet graduation still feels far off, and students may be putting too much focus on social activities. Encourage your teen to pursue their interests while maintaining focus on their goals. With your support, 10th grade will be your student's best year yet.

Conversation Starters

- How did you feel at the start of 9th grade and then at the end? What were some challenges and what did you learn from those challenges? How do you feel this year as a 10th grader?

- What are your classes this year? What goal do you have for each class, and which classes will require the most focus?

- Have you started thinking about what you would like to do after you graduate from high school? Are there any electives or advanced courses you want to take that would help you reach that goal? What can I do to help you stay focused on your goals?

- Which clubs or sports are you interested in joining? What about other activities that might interest you outside of school? What can we do at home that will help you balance schoolwork and club or sports activities and personal interests?

- This year you take the PSAT, plus there are other standardized tests you will take as a sophomore. How are you feeling about that? What do you need to do to prepare for those and how can I help you with that preparation?

- How involved do you want me to be and what kind of support do you need from me this year to help you stay focused, manage your time, and balance school and your personal life?

Chapter 2

HOW IS A 10TH GRADER DIFFERENT FROM A 9TH GRADER?

What to expect from your high school sophomore

Stacey Donaldson, PhD, NBCT
2010 Mississippi State Teacher of the Year

It would probably be difficult to find an expectant mother—or father, for that matter—who has not heard of or read *What to Expect When You're Expecting*, a best-selling pre- and postnatal book that details the gestational journey. It would have been nice to have had such a guide with my girls as they matured significantly during their teen years. Having taught both 9th and 10th graders, I know that these students resemble each other at first glance, but I'm happy to report that, after the summer between 9th and 10th grade, a more mature, independent, and focused sophomore has usually emerged.

Academic Maturity

Place a first- and second-year high school student shoulder-to-shoulder, and it's difficult to tell the difference, but there is a significant change in some students that becomes noticeable as the school years progress. The level of maturity is recognizable in some sophomores with their approach to academics. With lighthearted humor, I am thankful that all first- and second-year students are not the same. I have witnessed some freshmen sacrifice grades for appearance within their peer groups. For some freshmen, appearing careless about grades is a cool thing to do until it shows up on progress reports or results in failure. Not all freshmen took this route, but peer pressure is a driving force for this age group.

Preparation is a large part of the freshman year. Freshman students and their parents will hear many messages about the process of preparing for state tests. If a child is in an accelerated class like algebra, testing may have started as early as 8th grade. However, most subject-area tests begin during the 9th and 10th grades, which is one motivation for students to be better stewards of what they are learning academically.

Freshmen may have at least one state test requirement under their belts, but they are exposed to content and rigor that prepares them for sophomore state tests. I have witnessed freshmen who did not perform well take advantage of opportunities to do better in their sophomore year. From a teacher's perspective, the critical thinking skills freshmen sharpen in 9th grade allow sophomores to show up the following year with improved analytical thinking skills and creativity that they will use academically and socially.

Social Dynamics

Some students continue morphing into the social butterflies that adorn high school classrooms. High school is its own form of socialization, but social media adds to the dynamism of student interactions.

It takes maturity not to get sucked into chaos that originated online. I have seen sophomores handle issues by consulting with a teacher or parent, and it affirms that some students in their second year are better able to converse with adults for social troubleshooting.

Many high schoolers are also exploring their identity. Social media plays a role in this exploration, as students are exposed to other people of varying ages and cultural backgrounds that may open their eyes to different hobbies, fashions, and interests. It's quite interesting to look down the hall and see any number of shades of hair color or types of clothing. However, I have found that sophomores are getting closer to developing into the young adults they aim to be. The freshman with extremely green hair may have a more restrained look for their sophomore year. Identity exploration is often about freedom of expression and personal evolution.

Independence

Effective teachers communicate with students' families and strive to keep open communication throughout the school year to inform them when practice is needed and to partner with parents as necessary. Ideally, students are becoming better equipped to ask for help in areas of struggle instead of settling for poor performance. Some sophomores may even be more open to communicate with parents and take on more responsibilities at home and school. This behavior change is a welcome adjustment for parents and children.

During high school, students are responsible for setting their course schedule, with assistance from the school counselor. For this reason, you should have discussions with your teen at home about their interests and course selection. Counselors typically welcome questions from parents that can help them usher students into the appropriate selection of courses. Some students may choose the career and technical track, which has become easier as career academies are more prevalent in schools.

Depending on a student's schedule, sophomores can spend some of their day assisting in the office or serving classroom teachers. Though more common in 11th and 12th grades, I've seen sophomores express interest as they see upper-level students help out. Your sophomore may also want to get a part-time job to start having some financial independence. Again, this level of independence is an exciting adjustment for both parents and students and should be taken seriously.

Extracurricular activities become a haven for many students during their high school careers. Whether it's sports or the arts, some students are motivated to participate and have simultaneously learned how to be successful in both these extra activities and academics. I have noticed that less mature students are prone to focusing more on extracurriculars, which may mean their grades take a hit. Sophomores are starting to focus on college and scholarship potential connected to their extracurriculars, which is a good thing, as students are exposed to careers in school. They're beginning to think of ways to support themselves.

Time Management

As students move from one grade to the next, they must manage time more effectively. Sophomores continue refining their management skills to balance academics, extracurricular activities, and social and service activities.

All students are coming to grips with the importance of achieving balance necessary for success. While some students are better at time management than others, parents play a key role in helping students set boundaries. As mentioned, some sophomores may add a part-time job to their schedules, but they should understand that academics always take priority over work. It's important that students know it's okay to say no to opportunities that fill their time but may not serve them appropriately.

Future Interest

Students are more aware of the value of doing well on standardized exams like the PSAT, SAT, and ACT, even though many colleges and universities have gone test-optional since the pandemic. Parents should not be surprised if this awakening sometimes comes with distinct types of anxiety. Students are like sponges and hear what parents, teachers, and other significant figures say about college expenses, like:

- "I'm not paying for college."
- "I need you to score high enough on the ACT to get a full scholarship."
- "Jason made a 32 on his ACT! He will not have a problem getting scholarships."

These are statements that students can internalize, which ends up working against them. They may never acknowledge their fear of performance, but some students are afraid they will not do as well as their peers or older siblings. It is important to encourage students not to compare themselves to other students. "Run your own race" is good advice that helps remove unhealthy comparisons.

Sophomores are gaining exposure to community colleges and universities, which may act as further motivation to perform well in high school, because successful entrance into one of these institutions is riding on their high school record. Sophomores are looking at their older friends, some of whom are receiving entrance letters. I recall having to tell my daughter, who was concerned that she was not receiving acceptance letters when she was a sophomore, that it was too soon. Though sophomores are maturing, they still need parents' assistance to help them navigate this high school timeline.

Closing Advice

Sophomores can expect to find coursework a little more challenging, but it's nothing they can't handle thanks to their freshman year of preparation. Sophomores enter their year as experts, with lessons learned from their freshman year. Parents can expect to see many changes in their teens that force them to trust what their sophomores are capable of doing on their own, yet parents need to be standing close by to offer support and navigation assistance as students walk through their sophomore year, which promises personal growth and change.

Chapter 3
A DEEPER DIVE INTO COURSE SELECTION

What to ask your teen before they choose classes

David Bosso
2012 Connecticut State Teacher of the Year

Just before the start of a new school year, I received an email from a former student who had graduated several years prior. Maya wrote, "I appreciated your help growing up. You helped push me to try new things. I still remember being in your class and being engaged with what we were going to learn next." Her email went on to describe some of her accomplishments and activities, and it was clear that she was doing well. She stated that she was getting ready to start graduate school in the fall.

The timing of the email was perfect, as the summer was drawing to a close and I would be meeting and working with new students in a few days. The familiar sense of anticipation and excitement for staff and students was on the horizon. One of the greatest joys of teaching is getting to witness students strive, grow, and thrive. Teachers are fortunate because, during the course of a career, we have the opportunity to have a positive impact on the lives of thousands of students. There certainly is some truth to the expression that a teacher can never know where their influence ends. Sometimes, seemingly simple interactions can have far-reaching effects. A brief conversation about a student's interest and future plans, for example, can provide a foundation that builds confidence and serves to better focus post-high school aspirations.

Initial Conversations

Every year, as we turn the corner from winter to spring, we begin the process of course recommendations and registration. Many 9th grade students, who largely had their schedules set for them when they entered high school, are sometimes unsure about how to proceed when selecting courses among a wide range of possibilities. Course selection, while seemingly straightforward, is perhaps more daunting than one may realize, especially because credit requirements, types of courses, and career pathways have changed considerably over the years. Should students take more challenging Advanced Placement and honors courses? How should they decide the electives in which to enroll? What about a possibly increased workload and faster pace than what they have experienced during their freshman year?

During this time of year, I discuss with many students a variety of issues and challenges that they need to consider when thinking about course selection for their sophomore year. As their teacher, I am one of several individuals to whom they should reach out—along with other teachers, school counselors, parents or guardians, and fellow students who have experience with certain courses—who can provide a diversity of insights and a sense of what to expect, weighing the various factors that may come into play in the next phase of their academic experience. There are many variables to mull over, and teachers and others can offer practical, reasoned, and nuanced discernment, as well as pose questions to contemplate as students begin the registration process. Below are a few examples.

Are they truly interested in the topic?

Initially I ask a student why they want to take a particular course because I want to gauge their interest. Is it because their friends are taking the course? This might not be the best reason. At the same time, however, having a friend in the course might provide a level of comfort, especially if the course is made up of mixed grades or the students work well together and can help each other with the course concepts and studying. Other courses might be more appealing, and they can be more valuable than taking AP or honors-level courses, depending on student interest, who is teaching, or what teaching styles will be used. Is the student looking for a class in which they will be challenged and can grow academically? If so, your student should strongly consider registering for said class.

What additional factors come into play?

Other issues to keep in mind include whether the student has other responsibilities, commitments, and time constraints. Extracurricular activities, work at a part-time job, family obligations, or other responsibilities must be factored into any decision, as the time and energy required in their academic and social lives can easily be strained with too much on their plate. Will the student be taking multiple demanding, rigorous courses? If a student's schedule is filled with such courses, they can quickly become overwhelmed. Stress, lack of sleep, and limited leisure time can be physically and mentally detrimental.

Is 10th grade the right year to load up on advanced courses?

It might be best to start with, say, one AP or honors course during sophomore year in preparation for a more challenging course load in 11th and 12th grades. Too often, students drop a course early in the school year because the stark reality of course expectations becomes difficult to handle, and the resulting upheaval in the student's schedule becomes another stressor. If an AP course seems too intimidating, perhaps an introductory or survey version of the course exists, which can be an excellent gauge of interest and curricular demands.

Are they aware of the rigors of certain courses?

I also let students know that the pacing of a course, frequency of assignments, and overall workload might be something that they are not used to based on the experiences of their current year. There may be more notes, headier concepts, more challenging assessments, different strategies, and other aspects of a course that strain studying habits, learning skills, and organizational tactics. Some students may find that the challenges of a particular course may be the result of a larger class size or fewer supports and resources than for previous courses. Students should use the various strategies they have gleaned from preceding classes as they build their skill set—organization and time management tactics, preparation from assessments, graphic organizers, and more. There may be peer tutoring or after-school help available, and students should certainly ask their teachers for extra practice, clarification of course material and concepts, or other assistance.

Have you considered different teaching styles or assignments?

Even though the overall workload in advanced courses may be more challenging, other courses, including electives, may provide new and exciting experiences. Nontraditional assignments—which may be more hands-on, interdisciplinary, or available on different types of online platforms—might be entirely engaging and informative, stretching understanding and encouraging deeper analysis and interest. Some courses may be more lecture-based or more hands on. Some teachers, depending on pedagogical approaches or course content, grant more student autonomy than others. While students should not solely select a course because of who may be teaching it, some students perform better in certain classroom cultures than others. Bear in mind that what transpires in classrooms during the course of a semester or a year, while undoubtedly influenced by teachers, is to a certain extent dictated by the curriculum and other factors as well.

Finding the Balance

Students and parents may find it helpful to see a holistic view of the student's schedule—everything from the daily school schedule and routines to extracurricular activities, personal responsibilities, social events, and other obligations. A broader view will provide a keener understanding of the burdens of a heavy course load. In concert with teachers and counselors, parents/guardians have a good sense of what their child can handle, what might be aggravating factors in school or at home, how they handle successes and frustrations, their interest level, their skills, and their preparedness for certain types of courses. There is no benefit to gain from taking particular courses if other aspects of a student's life or family dynamics may be negatively affected. Consider your own and/or your co-parent's responses to schoolwork completion and grades.

Banking the Credits

Finally, your student needs to ensure they will earn the right number of credits by the end of their sophomore year. Staying on track to graduate, making sure that the proper course sequence is being followed, and checking that required courses are being taken should all be discussed with their school counselor, as well as post-high school and/or career goals. Some courses offer certification and/or real-world learning experiences that may go a long way toward building the confidence and competence of students as they consider certain careers. High school is an excellent opportunity to take advantage of the many experiences that are offered via coursework and otherwise (i.e., building connections with teachers, considering possible career paths, exposure to novel ways of learning). The range of courses offered at many high schools compared to the recent past is quite impressive—from gourmet cooking and technology to marine biology and criminal investigation—and a student would be hard-pressed *not* to find a course that piques their interest, expands their knowledge base, and helps them flourish as a learner.

Closing Advice

A few days after I received Maya's email, I thanked her and let her know how proud I am of her. I reflected on her time in my classroom and the interactions and conversations we had during her four years at our school. While I was not the only adult who played a role in influencing her decisions, including course selection, I know that my occasional pieces of advice about courses, college, and careers had an impact—perhaps even more than I initially realized. In my reply to Maya, I wrote, "I always knew you were destined for great things. I am thrilled, but not in the least bit surprised, that you have been so successful (and will continue to be!)." I also inquired about her plans for graduate school: What university would she be attending? What would she be studying? A few days later, she wrote back. Her future plans? Teaching!

Conversation Starters

- What are your interests, priorities, goals, and academic skill sets that may impact your experience in various courses, particularly more rigorous ones, such as AP and honors?

- What are your goals for after high school, and in what ways might they impact course selection?

- How familiar are you with your high school's program of studies, required courses, and elective offerings? How can I help in your course selection process?

- What types of learning environments, teaching styles, and course pacing work best for you?

- How do you think the way you handle challenges, setbacks, successes, and other experiences may affect your experience in various types of courses?

Chapter 4
INCLUSION AND BELONGING

How your teen finds their people

Al Rabanera
Algebra Teacher, California

The sound of the school bell ringing echoes through the halls as students begin to enter my classroom. These students started the year not new to the school, but new to my classroom. As they shuffle in, it's the small things I notice that help me identify how the students want to be perceived, ranging from their style of clothing (baggy pants or skinny jeans) and how the clothing is worn (high-waisted or sagging to expose their underwear) to accessories (earrings, nose rings, and various piercings; hats with different logos and sports team names; shoes), haircuts, and even their fingernails. Even the quick interactions that we have as I greet my students are a part of how they present themselves—it's how they want to be perceived by others, and their clothing is an expression of their self-image that makes lasting first impressions. These details are what I use to connect with my students, to develop rapport and create a sense of belonging in my classroom, and some of these same ideas can be used by parents to check in with their teens about how they are feeling connected to school.

Student Identity

As I walked around my classroom greeting my students, I noticed Adam's shirt had a graphic on it that I had never seen before. As it was challenging to make out what it said, I asked Adam about it. He told me it was a death metal band that he listens to and really likes. With my limited knowledge of death metal, I asked Adam if he understood the lyrics or if it sounded more like mumbling, growling, and shouting. Adam chuckled and told me that the music sounded more like mumbling and shouting and that you really could not make out the words to the songs. These types of conversations create opportunities for my students to feel "seen" and are important because they build trust and credibility, which helps to cultivate a sense of belonging and community in my classroom.

As students begin to self-identify, they tend to congregate around other students with similar mannerisms, shoes, shirts, and hairstyles. These students naturally gravitate to each other and begin to build community inside and outside the classroom. Knowing this, and also the fact that the students may already know each other from the previous year, I am intentional about how I use this information to create connections with my students. I take mental notes about what we talk about, so when opportunities and activities that may fit a student's interests come up, I can encourage the student to check those out or to reach out to the activity's advisor to get more information.

As a parent myself, I can empathize with wanting to understand how my teen fits in and how their self-identity impacts their sense of belonging in the classroom and at school as a whole. I often wonder how my own children act and behave at school versus at home. Here are some questions to reflect upon to better understand how your student can explore their identity:

- What are some of your teen's previous and current interests and hobbies?

- Have you checked your school's website to find information about the types of co-curricular or extracurricular activities that are available? Follow the school's social media and newsletter, as well, to see if any activities match up with your student's interests.

- Is your teen more quiet and keeps to themselves (an introvert) or more outgoing and likes to be around others (an extrovert)? Depending on the answer, suggest they email their counselor, career center, activities director, or staff at school about clubs they may be interested in.

- What are different strategies you can use to support your teen to engage in these activities?

Students in 10th grade more than likely have already found their friends from the previous year or have held onto friendships that reach back to middle or even elementary school. So, how do you know that your teen has begun to find where they fit in and feel comfortable? As your teen's interests begin to either develop and deepen or expand into new interests, how can you tell if your teen has found a safe space to fit in? Take a moment to reflect on the relationship that you have with your child, asking:

- What do you spend most of your free time doing and with whom?

- What are you most interested in learning and doing?

- What types of activities are you excited to actively participate in?

Your teen's friend groups share the same interests, hobbies, and colloquial language, creating a sense of belonging. Your student's identity is shaped and molded by this group of friends, even as their preferences may change as quickly as current trends. Remain mindful that your child notices your responses and reactions when they push boundaries as they explore their identity and perceptions of themselves. When pushing these boundaries begins to harm the child physically, emotionally, behaviorally, and/or socially, you should step in.

Finding Your People

Adam was new to our school when he joined my student leadership class. Initially, he appeared shy and quiet, and, to help break the ice, I grouped students together to plan and create school-wide activities to engage the student body. The more activities that Adam worked on, the more comfortable he became engaging with his classmates and working in class. Providing opportunities for students to cultivate relationships with each other allows them to develop rapport and trust with each other. From what I witnessed, the leadership class had become Adam's support system and he had found his "people" that he could relate to and confide in.

More than likely, your student has already developed a system of support with their friends to socialize and spend time with, to help cope with challenges, and to lean into when making choices about academic and personal decisions. If your student is new to the school like Adam was, or naturally introverted, it may take some time to form relationships while your teen becomes more accustomed to, or comfortable in, their classes and the school. The connections that your student makes with their classmates are created through shared experiences and struggles in the classroom as they persevere together through the learning process. In today's digital age, it may be even easier for students to connect with each other via various social media platforms or video games.

As a parent, I try my best to explicitly model support of my child by saying out loud how I found my people similar to the way they are making their own connections—sometimes that is what my child needs to hear to build confidence and feel validated. Think about what you are doing or what you can be doing to become a more active part of your student's support system and help them find their people. Some questions that you can ask yourself to learn more about your student and their support system are:

- How are you engaging with your teen to know that you are still in tune with their interests, hobbies, and passions?
- What can you do to stay informed and strengthen your relationship with the educators that are in most contact with your student? Do you regularly attend parent-teacher conferences? Do you participate in school events and parent workshops?
- Are you familiar with the co-curricular and extracurricular activities that are available at your student's school?
- How are you making opportunities to meet with your student's "people?"

Roles Students Play

Adam found his people at school and felt connected through the work that he was doing in student leadership. The students were active members of the class and had specific roles and responsibilities. Each one had a hand in helping move the work of the class forward. I taught the students to have very high standards for the work that they produced and to be proud of the work that they were doing because it was not only a representation of themselves, but also of their classmates and of our class as a whole. I encouraged my students individually and as they worked as a group to bring their best selves, reinforcing each day the idea of bringing positive vibes to class because their attitudes and actions directly impact the work we do. By consistently checking in with each of my students and reminding them about how their work impacted our goals, I created a sense of inclusion, purpose, and belonging in my classroom. Each day, I modeled for my students how to treat all students with respect, dignity, and fairness and gave equitable opportunities for each student to participate.

As a teacher and parent, I am always searching for different activities and strategies to model in my classroom and at home to be explicit about being more inclusive. I have learned that the best way to be more inclusive is to first listen and understand what my students and children are saying, rather than just waiting to respond or to continue pushing my ideas. So, I asked my students how they feel about how they belong in student groups, in class, and at school. Below are a handful of responses that stood out to me:

- "We get treated the same. I don't feel left out of anything."
- "What makes me feel included is when everyone is welcoming."
- "It's also nice when everyone is getting to know each other."
- "Learning new things makes me feel like I belong in the classroom. I feel like I belong here to learn new things."
- "When the teacher makes eye contact."
- "When people talk to me."

By cultivating my classroom community, my students feel like they are connected to other students. However, being connected to the school is a different feeling, because it means that students feel like part of the school's culture as a whole. When I created my student survey, I asked about this. Below are my students' responses about how they felt connected to the school:

- "I feel like the ones that want to be included are the ones that sign up for Associated Student Body and clubs."
- "I also feel included when I participate in activities and projects with other people."
- "When people talk to me that I've never seen before in my life."
- "When people talk to me."

Dating

Dating for high school students is complex on so many different levels because students are still trying to figure out who they are as people and what they like and do not like, while evolving and figuring out who they are and how they fit in. Like so many other students in my classes, Adam had connected with another student, and I noticed that the relationship moved beyond just being classmates. There are no hard and fast metrics to measure dating effectiveness and efficacy—like formative assessments and standardized testing scores—because dating can range from being just outside the friend zone to regularly talking to "seeing each other" to having an official title, depending on your student's perspective. From what I have seen as a teacher, the more that students have contact with each other, like being in the same classes and working together in groups, the more likely they will begin to develop friendships that may work themselves into a relationship.

From a parent's perspective, how does dating play into the narrative of inclusion and belonging? Your teen has been watching and learning social cues from interactions, conversations, and situations throughout their lives. As difficult as it may be, it is crucial that you are supportive of your student's relationships and provide guidance when asked for advice. Also, be mindful that unsolicited relationship advice may cause an adverse reaction from your teen. Some questions to ask your teen about dating could be:

- What do you know about consent and the word "no?"
- What do you consider a safe relationship, including being safe when it comes to sex?
- What have you learned about relationships from what you see at home?

Closing Advice

After settling in during 9th grade, sophomores are starting to form their student identity, find and solidify their friend groups, and maybe even start dating. It's important to stay connected to your 10th grader, while also letting them figure things out on their own. Validate their choices, model the type of behavior you'd like from them, and ask lots of questions! Remember that the school staff is there for you and your student, but try to let your sophomore take control in finding the right activities for their interests.

Chapter 5
THE DOS AND DON'TS OF SUCCESS

How to support your teen in the classroom

Chris Grouzes
2023 Pennsylvania National and State Teacher of the Year Finalist

"Don't slack off!" was the first answer, and it was uttered before I could finish the question. The question? Well…

Okay, here's how it went down. When my 10th-grade students came into my room today, the Bell Ringer (aka Do-Now, Opening Activity—basically, something for the students to do at the beginning of class) was a prompt that read:

> *"I am working on an essay. The goal of the essay is to offer parents advice about how to best support their 10th-grade students in the classroom. I think I have an idea of what to say, but I could use some help. Seriously, I need help. What advice would you give?*

- In your answer, please include examples of:
    i. Parallel structure
    ii. Proper use of a semicolon
- Work on your own first and put together a good pitch for your future partner."

For three minutes, I got to bask in the sweet, satisfying pitter-patter of student keyboards. Students vigorously typed. Then they'd pause to look up and around in deep thought. Then back to typing. Then they would stop to click around. Some were looking up a synonym, while others needed a refresher on parallel structure. The pauses did not last long, though. At the three-minute mark, my timer buzzed, and the class immediately broke up into pairs. After about a minute, it was time for full group discussion.

After the second timer went off, I said, "All right. Let's chat. So, what advice do you ha—"

"Don't slack off!" a student in the back excitedly shouted.

"Naaaah," another student said, while slouched in his chair (confident and alert, but passively slouched). "That's advice for students. Not their parents."

"Well," the first student clapped back with respectful sarcasm, "I'm tellin' parents…" He paused and smirked at his partner. His partner joined him, and they said in unison, "Don't put stuff off; don't do it for them," (pause) "don't expect too much."

Don't put stuff off; don't do it for them; don't expect too much.

First, let's take a moment to give the students props for absolutely crushing both semicolons and parallel structure. Oh, and it's brilliant—much more brilliant than these students realized. The class talked about it for another five minutes or so before we jumped back into chapter 2 of *Lord of the Flies*. The class moved on, but I had to scribble this tidbit onto a sticky note to ponder later.

I've pondered, analyzed, and used this pseudo-mantra as a rubric through which I've run a few pieces of my own advice. I call it a "pseudo-mantra" because the rhetoric leaves a bit to be desired. As much as I love the parallel structure and tricolon in the students' use of "don't," I try to give advice by trading out "don't language" for "do language." With that said, I appreciate the sentiment of what my students came up with so much that I've kept it here. You'll see that, throughout the chapter, I offer alternative wording for each.

So, from teacher to parent, by way of student, here are a few ideas to consider as you prepare your child for success in their 10th-grade classroom.

Let's address the elephant in every classroom first. I'm surprised I made it this far without mentioning it, but…we agree that the COVID lockdown was terrible, right? Remember what school was like during that time? As a teacher, I look back and literally (not figuratively—*literally*) shudder. As the world navigated the seemingly countless obstacles, many teachers and schools made a huge change that has proven to be sadly detrimental. Schools, teachers, parents, and students were justifiably in survival mode, which gave way to a new way of grading: finish the assignment when you can, and you'll receive full credit. This approach was born out of necessity, and it was supposed to be a temporary fix while we figured out, well, everything else. A big issue, though, is that, though the rest of the world tried to pause in hopes of "getting back to normal," young people didn't stop forming their understanding of the world around their immediate present. They learned that education was transactional and that there wasn't any gray area between the strict binary of success and failure.

Don't Put Stuff Off (Be Proactive and Invite Risk)

Encourage your student to take social risks. Encourage them to try on an assignment, even if they think they aren't going to do well on it. Encourage them to find and appreciate nuance in their school experience. If a student's perceived reality is that they can only go one way or another, they will only allow themselves to fall into one of the two predetermined options: success or failure. This leads to perfectionism without the capacity to struggle or persevere. Perfectionism leads to procrastination, because students don't want to start something if they can't do it perfectly. Perfectionism, procrastination, and a lack of experience with struggle is a recipe for catastrophizing and anxiety.

Failure leads to success

It's monumentally important to remind your 10th-grader that failure is not the opposite of success; it is an integral part of success. I'm not saying that school was easy before 10th grade, but I am saying that, many times, the jump in intensity is more significant from 9th to 10th grade than the one from 8th to 9th. In most districts, students change buildings, and many freshmen get some leeway, especially coming out of the version of school that happened during COVID. I'm not presenting this as a negative; I'm merely presenting it as an area of concern.

Failure and all its buddies—disappointment, sadness, regret, self-doubt, awkwardness, all those brands of discomfort, to name a few—are crucial ingredients to success. They are the foundation on which success needs to be built. If we build the success without the foundation of failure, we cannot fully appreciate it. Without the bitter, the sweet isn't as sweet. We need to experience one extreme to reach and appreciate the other. The longer we put off the bitter, and the more we keep our students from the bitter, the longer it will take them to experience the sweetest version of sweet. Or, if it takes too long for them to experience the bitter, they may have a much harder time finding their way to the sweet...or identifying the sweet when they earn it. Let them struggle. Let them earn that bitter foundation so they can enjoy their sweet success as they build it. It hurts, but any worthwhile growth does.

Promote self-advocacy

Another foundational skill that 10th-grade students should try to hone is self-advocacy. Though this isn't specific to 10th graders, it is especially important for this age group. Today, it's asking a teacher for help, but next year, it could be talking to potential colleges. Soon after, they will need to advocate for themselves at a job. Tenth grade is the perfect time to start to hand over, or at least share, the responsibility for communication with teachers, counselors, and administrators.

This may seem like a difficult skill to impart, but I have an approach that has proven to be helpful time and time again: open communication between your student, yourself, and the student's teachers. Send an email to each teacher, very briefly introducing yourself and your student. Copy your student on that email, and help them type out a simple "reply all," introducing themselves. This does three things:

1. It makes clear to all involved parties that your student is going to be in on these conversations.
2. It shows the teacher that you are a proactive, not reactive, parent.
3. It establishes that there will not be a "he said, she said" dynamic among these three parties, who are on the same team.

You aren't bothering the teacher by reaching out and saying hi. They will appreciate the kindness, and the positive result will set a good tone for your student's foray into self-advocacy.

Copy your student on every single communication that you have with their teachers. As the year progresses, and your student needs help but is anxious about approaching their teachers, encourage them to write an email to a specific teacher, with you copied, asking to stay after class for a second to ask a question. This reduces uncertainty about the situation, and it capitalizes on students' comfort with online communication. Use one skill to help build the other! This gradual release will offer your student a safety net as they learn to navigate email communication and self-advocacy. With this approach, you help your student persevere, but you avoid doing it for them. Wait, that's part two of our pseudo-mantra! Let's ride that segue.

Don't Do It for Them (Let Them Struggle)

Every struggle is an opportunity to grow. Celebrating growth with little check-ins encourages your student to value the process instead of relying on validation from the product. Gen Z is not the first generation to heed a product-driven personal reward system. It is the first, however, to experience the need for immediate gratification in the way that it does. See: smartphones, social media, Amazon, etc. When that need for immediate gratification hangs out with the perfectionism that we discussed earlier, and then they invite the student's product-driven philosophy, we have a stressful soiree that never quiets down.

Helping students find their own definition of success can help break the binary of success and failure. Their understanding of success may not be the same as yours or their teachers'. I'm not asking you to submit to their alternate view of success, but I am inviting you to have a conversation with your student, prior to starting 10th grade, that explores success as a fluid concept. Ask yourself a few questions before discussing with your teen:

- What does success look like to you as a parent?
- As a friend?

- What about success with regard to your job and/or lifestyle?
- Incremental growth is success, right?

The now-cliché term "helicopter parent" has become kind of a catch-all for a parent who keeps close tabs on their kid's education. I'm not accusing you of being a helicopter parent; I don't know you! Besides, most students benefit from extra parental support. Let's agree that there is a large, nuanced space between negligent and helicopter parents. All I'm saying is, the closer you are to your student's day-to-day education, the less likely they are to take risks and experience failure. If they are struggling and you squash the struggle, they won't be able to build the necessary tools to self-advocate in other aspects of their lives.

Don't Expect Too Much (Meet Them Where They Are)

No matter where your 10th grader stands as a reader, writer, speaker, mathematician, historian, scientist, athlete, artist, or anything else, they may run into the well-rounded student fallacy, which they should know is not a real thing. Years ago, colleges put out into the ether that they wanted students who were multifaceted, and that burned out Gen Xers and Millennials because we felt like we had to be involved with and in charge of everything. Colleges have changed their tune about that lately. Now, they are starting to value the students who are exploring an avenue that interests them, especially if it's related to their intended major. Think about your job. Did your boss want to hire you because of how good you are at what you do for the company or how good you are at a bunch of other stuff? Of course, it's nice to be well-rounded, but to have "well-rounded" as one's defining characteristic isn't unique, and it can prevent a student from realizing their fullest potential because they are dedicating their time to so many other things.

If your student is college-bound, then 10th grade is a great time to start thinking about taking the PSAT or practice ACT. When parents call my tutoring company to ask for test prep, I urge them to avoid the test until December of sophomore year, at the earliest. And students should try to have the test in their rearview mirror by September of their senior year. I mention this here because I want to invite you to let your student take their time when signing up for these tests. The tests are super-stressful, even with several colleges and universities going test-optional, and your student has plenty of time to work on studying. Structure it, though! A good barometer of when to have them take the test is whenever they are taking Algebra II. If they take the test before they take Algebra II, they will struggle more than they need to.

Regardless of how much school and standardized test boards try to create a norm, there is no one way to educate or be educated. There's not a specific pace that is standard for all students. Meeting students where they are does not mean letting them take the wheel. Meeting them where they are just asks us to zoom out and look at the whole person, not just the 10th grader. The whole person and the 10th grader aren't mutually exclusive, but they aren't synonymous, either. Around 9th or 10th grade, there can be a conflation of these two ideas that can lead to a student, with the binary way of thinking that we discussed before, believing that, because they struggle in school, they are struggling as a person. In extreme cases, this conflation leads students to either get so caught up in school that they are anxious all the time and become hypervigilant about "succeeding" in school, or, well, they get caught up in school and get anxious, but they shut down out of overwhelm and it reads as laziness.

Closing Advice

This age group is vulnerable and curious. They are on the precipice of defining who they are going to be as young adults, and we should approach their education with this in mind. Checked boxes and test scores do not define a person in the adult world. Effective communication, perseverance, and identifying nuance are some of the most important things for 10th graders to gain from their time in school. If you look back at the Bell Ringer and ensuing discussion at the beginning of this chapter, you'll see that I talk to my 10th graders like they are real people whose opinions matter to me. Because they are—and they do. You hopefully saw that I wasn't putting on a show for my students. I wasn't trying to impress or intimidate them. By 10th grade, students can see through that. I hold very high standards for my students, but I do so by challenging them to grow as people. The content is just a means to do that. Tenth grade isn't just about having the correct answer; 10th grade is when analysis, social consciousness, and self-actualization move into the top skills that a student will need to succeed.

> ### Conversation Starters
>
> - How could building a habit of respectful self-advocacy benefit your school life?
> - What are some variables that affect your day-to-day life in school and at home?
> - Describe a "sweet success" you experienced that was built on a "bitter foundation."
> - What is your version of the happy medium between an uninvolved parent and a "helicopter parent?"

Chapter 6
FAILING FORWARD

How to support your teen in handling academic setbacks

Heidi Crumrine
2018 New Hampshire State Teacher of the Year

When my daughter was in third grade, she came home from school one day and described a learning challenge she faced in class. She was building a solar cooker in a small group as a part of a unit on solar energy and in her retelling she started with: "We had to try a few times to figure it out, but we just kept failing forward."*

"What does that mean? To fail forward?" I asked her, unfamiliar with the phrase, but intrigued.

"Oh, it means we use our mistakes to figure out what to do." I was stunned. As a high school teacher for nearly 15 years at that point, I had never heard a better description of the entire purpose of learning: Learning is the process, not the end goal, and the mistakes we make along the way are all a part of that process.

Learning is Messy

We don't want to see our children struggle, but the reality is, no matter what, your child will face an academic setback at some point in high school. For some students, this will be a bigger challenge than for others, but it is not something that anyone can avoid. And that's okay.

When your 10th grader struggles, they have you in their corner to help them navigate, whatever the challenge. That doesn't mean that you fix it for them, but you can guide them so that they develop the skills to handle this independently in the future. Further, if I may be so bold, I'd say that if your high schooler does not face an academic struggle at all in high school, then I wonder if they are being appropriately challenged in their schooling. Learning is messy, and there should be failure along the way.

The goal of high school should not be to get perfect grades all of the time. It should be to try new things and be supported in growing independence and skills that will set a young person up to succeed as an adult. That is no small task, because we are talking about 15- and 16-year-olds who very much want to be seen as adults who no longer need their parents. Parenting this age group can feel so personal, because when our teenager rejects what we are offering, it feels like they are rejecting us—which often leads to conflict. Rarely does this rejection have anything to do with you, so don't take it personally. As the mother of a 15-year-old myself, I know this is easier said than done.

Learning Becomes More Difficult

As a teacher who has worked with both 9th and 10th graders for 20 years, I have observed that 10th grade is often when students begin to struggle in their coursework. There could be a variety of reasons for this, but 10th grade is often the year when students begin to take more advanced or specialized courses. The newness of high school has worn off, and the reality that there are three challenging years ahead has sunk in. When this happens, we often see students losing confidence and questioning their abilities. As our first line of defense in supporting our 10th graders, regardless of the root problem, our message needs to be that **this is normal, learning is hard,** and **it is okay to fail forward.**

For a motivated student who has always (and often easily) gotten good grades, this can come as a shock to the system. They have likely wrapped up their good grades as a part of their identity and have felt pride in always being seen as a good student. They also might start to see their longtime friends achieve at higher academic levels, making it feel to them like they are no longer equals. Suddenly, their own achievement is not happening as easily, and they might start to question their self-worth.

For a student who has always struggled, this comes as a different shock to the system. While they might have just gotten by or been able to fly under the radar, by 10th grade, gaps in their skills might become more apparent and prevent them from completing their coursework. Often, a student who has masked weak reading or math skills by always working with a friend, for example, is no longer able to do this. This student might also question their self-worth.

The Importance of Buy-In

The most important part of working with a 10th grader who is struggling is that **they need to buy in.** They are not adults, and their brains are not fully developed yet, but they are the ones who are going to succeed or fail. This may require flexibility in your parenting that you had not expected. Remember that this is not about you and your expectations; it is about what is best for your child. If you come from a family where everyone goes to college, for example, hearing your teen say that they are interested in a different path is not so easy. But it may be the most successful one for your child.

I have found that struggling students can come in many forms, but they often fall into three common groups:

	What does the issue look like?	What might it feel like?	What is the behavior like?
Group 1	• One class is a major struggle. • One skill or assessment is a major struggle.	• Student feels lost in one particular class and, no matter what they do, they can't catch up. • Student redoes work, and it is still wrong. • Student tries on homework and tests and thinks they did okay, but get the work back and they did not do well. • Lifetime friends are finding the class easy or at least not so hard, so there is a sense of shame or embarrassment. • Student thinks they are the only one who is struggling.	• Normal functioning: Worry is confined to the class. • Student might announce they don't like the class or the teacher "doesn't like" them.

(continued)

Group 2	• Many classes are a struggle. • Attendance issues, but only for certain classes.	• Student is still coming to school every day. • Student can see that they are having success in some areas. • Student is still connected at school and engaging in sports, music, or other extracurriculars.	• Class avoidance: student might skip or feel sick and need to be dismissed.
Group 3	• No academic success in any classes. • Student may attend school but not go to class, attend classes but do no work, or not attend school at all.	• Student feels horrible but can't see a way out. • Student maintains friend relationships, but no longer does school. • Student starts to see divide between friends who are succeeding and themselves, and they feel worthless.	• There can be a range of behaviors; student can look withdrawn or defiant. • Class attendance and work completion are down to zero.

How we support our 10th grader should depend on what they need and in what ways they are struggling. There is no one-size-fits-all approach to helping a struggling student, just like there is no one-size-fits-all approach to life. Consider the following approaches, depending on what your child needs:

Group 1

Description

This is a student who has an idea of what they want to do with education, but the academics are simply getting too hard. This often happens with a class like chemistry or physics, where the combination of conceptual and mathematical theories all at once can lead to confusion. It can also happen if a student is in the advanced section of a math class and things seem to just be moving too fast.

Your Role

Your role in this situation should be behind the scenes. You do not need to email the teacher or try to solve the problem for your child. Ask your student to email the teacher and describe what is happening. This is a wonderful opportunity for them to practice self-advocacy and connect with their teacher. You can follow up with the school counselor and the teacher to see if the student made contact, and you can ask how it is going, but wait a bit before doing this.

Your student needs to be supported in understanding how close they are to returning to a feeling of success. Often, 10 minutes a day or week of teacher time outside of class is enough to get them back on track. They also need to understand that teachers love students who are trying to learn what they are teaching. It's also important that the student understands that they didn't do anything wrong; learning is hard, and this is a part of that.

You should be *guiding* more than *doing*.

Student Buy-In

Students in this situation are generally motivated to get back on track. Their buy-in is a desire to get the grades they want.

Group 2
Description
This student needs more parental and school support but is capable of turning things around with that support. This student likely knows what they want for their education, but they have become overwhelmed with what that might mean and have started to avoid the hard things as a result.
Your Role
You will be taking a more active role than what you might like, but your child needs it. Many parents I have worked with in this role have tried to back off their interventions (like checking grades and attendance) to give their child some responsibility. They often feel guilty, as though this is their fault, or they are angry that their child didn't step up to the plate. Let both of those emotions go. This is not your fault, and your child is not a disappointment. They are just 15 years old.
You should start with the guidance counselor to see if there are supports available. Schools often have guided study halls, academic centers, check-in/check-out programs, or mentoring designed to support students in this exact situation.
At this point, it is okay for both you and your student to email teachers for information and updates. You should include your child in the emails to teachers, and request that they do the same in their own correspondence.
You should see yourself as a part of a team that includes your child, but your goal should be to back off as your child finds success so that you are guiding more and doing less.

(continued)

Group 2 (continued)

Student Buy-In

Students in this position likely want to get back on track but are frustrated, overwhelmed, and/or embarrassed. They might not want to attend a meeting with you and their teachers, but they will come (albeit grumpily). They might resist the idea of attending academic support sessions, but they will go. They tend to turn their resistance around once they see small successes.

Student buy-in can often be tied to academic eligibility for an extracurricular activity, a particular academic program at school, or the ability to have a job, car insurance discount, or another tangible goal that requires decent grades.

Group 3
Description

This student is at a crossroads. This crossroads could lead to a complete academic turnaround in the exact classes they are taking right now, but you and your student need to be prepared for that not to happen. This student likely does not know what they want for their education and is questioning what role academics play in their life. They will need coaching on what goal they are working toward, and they will need to be invested in whatever that goal is.

(continued)

Group 3 (continued)

Your Role
Parent involvement needs to be high at this point, but the student still needs to be involved as much as they can. You will need to be the one to coordinate meetings with the right adults and seek outside support as needed. Most often, this means adjusting their schedule. Possible outcomes could include dropping classes that are hopeless and looking into extended learning opportunities through the school, alternative programs, online coursework, or even programming at the local community college. There are often many less traditional opportunities available to high school students, but you might not know about them. Don't be afraid to ask. Your child's guidance counselor and teachers want your student to be successful and are willing to work with anyone who wants to try. It is appropriate at this point for you to contact and even meet with teachers or the counselor independently of your student.

Student Buy-In
At this point, student buy-in is often tied to an ability to stay in school and/or graduate, possibly on time. Eligibility for things like trade school, the military, or a specific job are tied to high school completion.

Perfection Should Not Exist

Lastly, a note about perfection. Too often, students wrap their self-worth up in their grades. They see their good grades as a reflection of who they are as human beings, and, as a result, when those grades aren't perfect, then neither are they. They worry because they see a society that places high value on grades. They worry about getting into just the right college, getting a scholarship, or becoming valedictorian. As teachers and parents, we inadvertently play into this by rewarding high grades and awards, which can be wonderful for many students, but this kind of praise can also shift their focus away from learning toward a sense of perfection at all costs. They don't need to reassess every single assignment so that they get the highest grade. In many ways, grades don't matter if students have worked hard, tried their best, and grown their skills and knowledge base.

I am not suggesting that we eschew all grades—that's a larger conversation for another day—but when we tie our praise and, thus, our students' sense of self-worth to a number, we are sending the message that when they struggle, they are not enough. The truth is that in life, we will struggle. There is no such thing as perfection, and those who seek perfection, not progress, are setting themselves up for a whole host of other struggles as they head into adulthood.

Closing Advice

My suggested message to all students is simple: You matter regardless of your success. Success is an arbitrary social construct that is deeply rooted in our capitalistic society. You need to work hard and try your best and find your own path toward happiness, not someone else's. We're here to help you figure that out along the way. Let's fail forward together.

Conversation Starters

- Does this class concept feel hard because it's new and you need to practice, or because you don't know what's going on or where to start?

- How do your teachers suggest you connect with them for extra help?

- Are you frustrated because you didn't get a perfect grade, or because you missed a key concept?

- Is this something worth stressing over because you'll need to apply it later, or is it something you can let go?

- How would you like me to offer support when you seem frustrated?

Chapter 7
DIFFERENT LEARNING STYLES AND ACCOMMODATIONS

What to do if you notice your teen working hard but struggling

La-Shanda West, EdS
Miami-Dade County Public Schools

Children are different. As a parent of three boys—ages 31, 15, and 9—I've noticed they each have unique abilities and interests, move at different speeds, and consume knowledge using various modalities.

My oldest son grew up when movies, snacks, and nap time were a part of the daily routine for kids in pre-K through early-elementary grades. Learning was more exploratory and mostly in the control of the teacher, with parental reinforcement through educational TV programs like *Mister Rogers' Neighborhood* and *Sesame Street,* which tapped into sound repetition and movement, as well as how to engage kids in the world around them. Children had limited experience with technology beyond the television. These shows reinforced basic skills like how to interact with peers and learning through songs and rhymes. They showed that learning does not necessarily require children to be sitting at a desk. A balanced approach to learning, along with age-appropriate television shows, afforded my oldest son a solid foundation in school. But he grabbed a basketball and football every chance he could. He played for the local YMCA basketball league, as well as Pop Warner football. He hit a brick wall in high school when the coach benched him because he was going hard on the court, but his grades were barely satisfactory. Coach reminded him: "You are a student-athlete; as such, your grades (learning) comes first, then sports." It was a challenge to change his mindset from athlete to student-athlete.

My 15-year-old sophomore is completely the opposite. He doesn't have a thirst for athletics. Instead, he is an illustrator and tech kid. He loves drawing cartoon characters and playing video games. He has been an illustrator since he was in elementary school. His artwork has earned him awards and he attends a magnet arts school.

Both my oldest and middle sons were exposed to high-intensity courses. My oldest wasn't placed in accelerated courses until middle school. My middle child was introduced to the International Baccalaureate (IB) program in the first grade. Ensuring that children are being intellectually challenged by introducing them to a rigorous education is beneficial, yet it poses a degree of pressure. As a parent, *you* should know what is in the best interest of your child and, together with your student's teachers, you should determine the educational track your child should take.

However, if your student is struggling and intervention is necessary, the school system is one of your most important allies in identifying whether they require screening for services in school, as well as sharing what strategies work for students with no federally mandated individualized plans. There is a misconception that if a child does not have an individualized education plan (IEP) or a 504 plan, the education system uses standardized test scores to deem them proficient or learning deficient. Luckily, educators understand that each student has strengths and areas of deficiency. Students struggle during the learning process for reasons both within and beyond their control, and they need a learning system that provides continuity at school, home, and in the community. If stakeholders are not invested in a soft approach to education, where each learner is treated as the most valuable pupil (MVP) in the school system, students will be disengaged in the learning process. As a result, student performance at school, and on district, state, and national assessments, will reflect their inability to master grade-level content.

Learner-Centered Classrooms

Why the shift to learner-centered classrooms? I can remember my early professional development trainings when I started teaching in 2001. Classroom management was the key to creating a positive learning environment. Daily practice included a routine schedule, working students bell to bell. A part of this process was creating a clear agenda, with activities to introduce the lesson, transition to the main classwork, then provide a wrap to the lesson, such as an exit ticket or reflection. The education system has come a long way since then. **Learner-centered classrooms** now actively involve students in the planning and instructional delivery of lessons. The shift teaches students **personal responsibility** and **self-advocacy**. Teachers are charged with meeting learners where they are and building upon their academic and social skills.

By 10th grade, the student, parent, and teachers should have a conversation intended to gather information about the following:

1. What do you, as the learner, need?

2. How can teachers effectively incorporate your interests in the classroom?

3. How have you connected to teachers and/or each subject matter in the past?

4. What is the most effective way you learn?

5. What are your strengths and weaknesses? (This may include but not be limited to facilitating group discussions, peer-to-peer support, reading, technology, writing.)

These questions allow your student to share basic information about how they learn.

Red Flags

When students are working hard yet struggling, there are signs to look out for before they get to the breaking point. It is critical that parents and teachers keep a running record of issues, like low grades or missed assignments, to diagnose the problem. Problems cannot be resolved unless there is evidence the problem exists and persists. By 10th grade, students know which subjects spark their interests. Although having the right teacher can make the difference, students who are mathematically skilled may calculate well without additional support. However, your student can master each subject but still fall short due to testing anxiety or other variables that may hinder their comprehension.

During 10th grade, students are faced with tough decisions. Am I college-bound? Am I ready to join the military? What are my career choices? While facing these questions, students are also expected to compete nationally in reading, science, and history. The National Assessment of Educational Progress (NAEP), referred to as "the nation's report card," along with state standardized assessments, collects and tracks data to monitor and compare pupil progression by district, state, and country. NAEP and other standardized assessments presume every student in grades 4, 8, and 12 to perform at or above grade-level mastery. But many students who take standardized tests struggle with test anxiety, which affects their mental health. Standardized test scores determine course placement for remedial, grade-level, and accelerated courses. Know your rights as a parent! Opting out of testing is one good solution. Another idea: assessments in the form of a portfolio, which can give a wider view of a student's academic performance. Meet with the school counselor and administration to discuss what alternatives to testing are available. There are so many reasons students struggle and are ready to give up; don't let standardized testing be one of them.

Learning Mediums

Learning mediums are tools necessary for active learning in the classroom, at home, and within community support organizations. Imagine a classroom of 25 impressionable minds. Each pupil has unique abilities as well as challenges. How can teachers tap into each student's abilities to build upon their strengths while also supporting their needs? This is when that running record of observable academic performance and student behavior and engagement, beyond report card grades, is vital!

Learning mediums can include:

> **Teacher instructions**, which are used in a large group setting, in small groups based on intervention needs, or one-on-one. If your student is struggling and is on the verge of giving up, ask for access to the teacher's instructions. This allows you to support your student at home, using the teacher as a resource.
>
> **Interactive technologies**, which can engage a student in learning through the use of technology. Decide which technological device is best for your teen. Paper and pencil is the ideal way to engage a learner in terms of accessibility and affordability. However, 21st-century learning requires your student to be a

digital learner. Since the COVID pandemic, most school districts provide devices for students to use at and outside of school. My 15-year-old's computer is set up for multitasking—academics, writing, drawing, and sketching. Find out what types of software your teen may need before purchasing your own home device. Not every parent may have the financial means to purchase a high-functioning device, and your teen may not need one.

Learning Barriers

You want to help support learning. When there are barriers to learning, you must take immediate action. The longer your student struggles in school, the sooner they become disengaged. The following are some common barriers and suggested solutions:

Learning Management System

Your school district's choice of learning management system (LMS), a platform essential for instruction and student learning, might be Edmodo, Microsoft Teams, Google Classroom, K12 (Stride), or Schoology. If your child is struggling with how to engage in the different functions of your school's LMS, email a school administrator to request parent training so you can have access and learn how to navigate the LMS with your teen.

Learning Styles

In 1997, Harvey F. Silver, Richard Strong, and Matthew J. Perini wrote about a learning styles theory concentrating on learning as a personal, individual act of thought and feeling. I like to focus on three types of learning styles:

> The **interpersonal learner** concentrates on information exchanged peer-to-peer or student-to-teacher. Effective communication is key, with open discussion and debate.

The **mastery learner** retains information delivered chronologically. Each step connects to the next, making learning logical and practical. The mastery learner requires learning beyond theory or textbook application and seeks to make sense of information through reasoning. The mastery learner requires content to be delivered in time, date, or sequential order.

The **self-expressive learner** uses visualization techniques to solve problems, examine probable solutions, and evaluate alternatives to the given problem.

Do you know how your student learns best? What is their preferred learning style? Students who are empowered to use their voices will be willing to tell a teacher what works for them and what does not. This really matters! Students must be at the center of the learning process. Understanding the notion that one size does not fit all is why it is important for parents to promote this self-advocacy. Students who self-advocate tend not to view "giving up" as an option. It is never too late to teach your teen how to self-advocate, especially when it comes to how they learn and retain information.

Mindset Matters

Sophomore year is a critical time for students. This is when students take rigorous courses, such as Algebra II and Chemistry, as well as accelerated courses like Advanced Placement, honors, International Baccalaureate, or Cambridge International—not to mention sitting in a classroom for 55 minutes to two hours at a time, depending on the bell schedule. Students attend school for six to seven hours (or more) each day, with limited time for one-on-one support or remediation with the teacher. To foster a willingness to learn, especially when it is challenging, **an educational mindset** is one of the solutions. This means finding value in the learning process beyond "I am learning because I have to learn." Parents must see value in learning beyond the classroom by fulfilling their role as invested stakeholders. Students who struggle will not give up if the educational mindset is reinforced at home. Even more importantly, teachers must embody an educational mindset. This requires teachers to identify the strengths that each student possesses and use these strengths as a way to reach and teach each pupil. As mentioned on page 58, students learn through their different styles, using various mediums (i.e., auditory, kinetic, technological, visual).

Create an environment where students value and feel empowered to have control over their educational experience. The first place to start is asking the struggling student open-ended questions, such as:

1. What do you feel is the purpose of education?

2. What kind of classroom would support your learning style?

3. What does academic learning look like for you?

4. How can we (parents and teachers) help you find value in the education system?

Resilience

How can adults build resilient children? In recent years, trauma-informed practices have been at the forefront of education policy. Trauma impacts children cognitively and emotionally. In order to identify a student's cognitive and emotional needs, schedule an appointment with a school counselor or psychologist when professional services are required. At a basic level, children have the capacity to understand and identify their level of resilience when dealing with life's challenges. Have yours take this quiz!

Resiliency Quiz

Rate each statement from 0 (never) to 5 (almost always).

1. I set goals and take the necessary steps to achieve them.
2. I don't give up easily when the going gets tough.
3. I am self-motivated.
4. I value myself, acknowledging my uniqueness.
5. I am a proud product of my family and community.
6. I balance my hobbies and other personal interests with school and home duties.
7. I have a hopeful mindset about the future.
8. I practice wellness and self-care.
9. I have the courage to self-advocate.
10. I know how to deal with difficult situations.
11. I trust adults who are a part of my support system.
12. I enjoy serving others.
13. I am receptive to perspectives not in alignment with my own.
14. I am flexible.
15. I am disciplined.
16. I am determined.

> 17. I use setbacks as opportunities to practice a growth mindset.
> 18. I am not afraid of learning new information.
> 19. I complete each task.
> 20. When situations get difficult, I persevere.
>
> Key: 0-25 (work with your teen to build up their resilience); 25-50 (remind your teen that they can self-advocate); 50-75 (your teen is almost there…); 75-100 (congratulations, your kid is resilient!)

Intervention

Educating a child requires the village to be invested. Creating systems of stakeholders to provide services for intervention when a student is struggling helps address the issues. The first system is the grade-level or intervention team at school. This intervention team includes:

General education and/or **special education teachers**, each of which possesses an area of expertise and can provide academic support before, during, and after school. A **school counselor** can provide social-emotional and coping strategies. Some students struggle because of stress and fear of failure. School counselors are critical when it comes to matters beyond academics—the realm beyond the teacher's control. An **administrator for curriculum and instruction**—the school site expert on best practices to support struggling students—can offer strategies for the intervention team and training on current evidence-based research to support the team.

The second system is **the parent** and **community**. Why do community partnerships matter when it comes to providing services to struggling students? They are stakeholders in education. There is a sense of shared responsibility—from parents choosing to live in a specific neighborhood because it has "good schools" with a safe reputation to public and private-sector businesses that give back to the community.

- The National Parent Teacher Association (PTA), in partnership with the National Education Association, is a community partnership that provides parents with guides to assist children with study habits and social media etiquette. It also offers wellness and time management strategies to help students as they face new academic concepts, extracurricular activities, and social pressures. See more at pta.org/home/family-resources/family-guides.

- The U.S. Department of Education Statewide Family Engagement Centers (SFEC) program provides financial support to assist organizations in effective family engagement policies, programs, and activities. The main goal of SFEC programming is to improve student development and academic achievement. Find out more at oese.ed.gov/offices/office-of-discretionary-grants-support-services/school-choice-improvement-programs/statewide-family-engagement-centers-program.

- The U.S. Department of Education funds national programs beyond the SFEC. Each school district receives funds from the department to assist with academic services that may include before- and after-school tutoring. Schools usually have an advisory committee to discuss program funding.

Closing Advice

No matter the age, a child struggling in school needs parental support. The student needs reassurance that they are capable and able to perform the tasks at hand. If the task is too challenging, self-advocacy is important. Having an open and honest conversation helps. You are the most important trusted adult in your high schooler's life, because you listen without judgment and offer love and support whenever it is needed. Know that you are not alone; your village is there to help. Be open to feedback from the teacher, counselor, and school administrator. When everyone works together, your teen has a greater chance to succeed.

Chapter 8

CHALLENGING STUDENT-TEACHER RELATIONSHIPS

How to know when to step in and help your teen

Renee Jones
2023 Nebraska State Teacher of the Year

Imagine two scenarios. In one, your student admits that they're frustrated with their teacher, or you deduce the anger through a series of emotionally driven interactions. For instance, you arrive at school pickup only to find your student fuming. Whether the interaction was first or last period, it doesn't matter—your student is visibly upset. The kind of upset that leaves them heavily sighing the moment the car door opens; perhaps you can already see the tears welling up in their eyes. The second situation is one where you can tell something is up. However, your teen volunteers no information. Maybe they are sitting there quietly, making deep sighs. Maybe they slammed the door. Either scenario tells you something happened in school today. Eventually you get it out of your student that they are having problems with a particular teacher.

Establish Safety

First and foremost, establish safety. Questions about safety, either physical or mental, may get you an eye roll or a "Mom, no!", but it is, of course, always essential to rule out this possibility. This conversation may be challenging, yet it is necessary. You might ask:

- What does safety mean to you—both physically and mentally? Do you feel safe at school and/or in that classroom?
- What is the name of a supportive adult you feel comfortable talking with at school?
- What does being in that classroom, or around that teacher, feel like to you?
- Do you feel respected by your teacher?
- What emotions did you feel during your interactions with the teacher?
- Are there any peers or teachers who pick on you or make you feel uncomfortable? Tell me about that.

Pause and Assess

After safety is established, I encourage you to fight the urge to immediately respond. Pause and fully assess the situation or what you know of the situation. In your assessment, include what you know to be true about your child and the relationship that may be pre-established between yourself and your child's teacher. Keep in mind that the lesson provided at the end of this scenario is most likely more important than automatically confirming that your child is "right" or, of course, that the educator is, by default, correct.

What is your end goal? What skill would you like your student to have learned from this scenario? While you may default to making phone calls and/or walking into the school to chat with the teacher, I remind you that your teen is only a few short years from needing to navigate these situations without you close by. This time it's a teacher; in the future it may be a professor, boss, or mentor. How can you use this moment as a lesson to increase the executive functioning skills of your student? Can you use it as a guide for a future moment when they will be navigating similar situations on their own?

Listen Without Judgment

Spend some time listening to understand. Keep in mind that what may be classified as a huge deal to your student may not feel like a big deal to you. The largeness of the issue isn't for you to decide. Their feelings, at this moment, are true for them. As a parent wanting to keep the doors of communication open, you must believe their experiences and their emotions as they present them, not as you believe they should feel.

Next Steps

Next, I would simply ask, "What do you need from me?" Invite your teen to:

1. Tell you if they'd like you to be a sounding board for a solution they've already settled on.

2. Ask you to walk them through their options of next steps.

3. Let you know they aren't sure of what to do and would like you to handle the situation.

Presenting your teen with options provides them the opportunity to begin to trust their inner voice, the one which is helping build the confidence to make decisions both large and small. Whatever their response, respect it.

1. Your Teen Chooses to Handle It

If your teen asks for you to let them handle it, simply say "okay, yes," even if it is incredibly difficult to do so. Provide your teen the opportunity to role-play the discussion as a way to build their confidence, and be a sounding board for any questions they may have. Encourage them to walk through the discussion, thinking about appropriate times and places to speak with their teacher. While listening, consider using open-ended statements such as:

- Tell me more about when you'll have this conversation.
- What information do you want your teacher to walk away with?
- What solution or resolution are you looking for?

Using leading suggestions allows your teen to hold the reins, while also providing reflection on the upcoming conversation. Assure your teen that you're there to listen and help, should their response ever change. Consider a follow-up in the coming hours or days to ensure that is, in fact, what they'd like to do, but, ultimately, show them you trust them.

If at any point you feel as though the situation warrants intervention because of safety, I'd continue with the steps below.

2. You Provide Some Options

When suggesting "I have a few ideas of ways to handle this. Would you like to hear them?", keep your preestablished lesson in mind. Ask open-ended questions, with the goal of guiding your student into making their own decision and figuring out their next steps and their feelings about it. Then follow up with a simple "What is your next step?" This helps your teen build their confidence in navigating tricky situations. Ultimately, we want them to learn to analyze a situation, assess the problem, and determine the next steps. Consider telling an anecdote from a similar situation from when you were in high school, one that may make them feel less alone or that they didn't totally screw something up.

A few questions that can help give your teen some options are:

- Do you feel comfortable discussing this with me, or is there someone else you'd rather talk to?
- How can I support you in this situation? Would you like to hear my thoughts, or do you prefer to handle it on your own?
- It is completely okay if you want to manage this yourself, but I'm always available if you change your mind. How would you like to proceed?
- Would it be helpful if we brainstormed some solutions together, or do you have a plan in mind already?

3. You Handle It

Do not assume that your teen already has the executive functioning skills needed to handle every situation. While they may pick up what adults, including you, do in similar situations, that alone isn't enough to assume your teen should just know how to handle something between themselves and their teacher. These life skills need to be taught, experienced, and then reflected upon.

So What Does All of this Look Like in Practice?

Consider the types of situations you're comfortable with guiding your teen through and which ones fall into the safe vs. unsafe categories, and, of course, the *yes, this child is nearly an adult but they aren't an adult and therefore I need to intervene* topic.

Situations you may feel comfortable letting your student work out on their own

With a few open-ended questions providing an opportunity for insight and reflection, the below situations are likely only a short conversation with the teacher away from being resolved:

- Frustration with a grade they received in class
- Refusal of a hall pass, when they felt it was necessary that they leave the room
- Clarification about an assignment
- Frustration with having to turn in their cell phone/AirPods
- Detention because of frequent tardiness
- The requirement of one-on-one interaction to purchase homecoming or other school event tickets
- Asking for help in or outside of class
- Being asked to move assigned seats
- Clarification on how to sign up for a sport/club/school-sponsored activity

Listening and validating your student's feelings and talking through these situations is a great opportunity for you to ask, "What do you believe is the solution or outcome that would resolve your emotional discomfort?" or "What's your next move?" Then simply have the courage to allow your student to work through and execute those next steps on their own. If they feel apprehensive, try to role-play the conversation. But let your teen steer the ship.

Situations you may want to consider guiding your student through

In addition to the abovementioned open-ended questions that lean into developing a better understanding, followed by reflection, ask your child about their desired outcome and what might the tangible next step be. The scenarios below may benefit from a detailed talk-through or practice:

- Feelings of being bullied (vary, dependent on the level of bullying)
- Wanting to change their current schedule
- Needing a mediation with another student in the same class
- Reacting to a family situation that your student says has a direct impact on their schoolwork
- Organizing their homework/planner
- Falling behind or needing an extension on an assignment
- Not wanting to sit near a student next to whom they do not feel productive
- Establishing systems to come to class prepared (i.e., charged Chromebook, appropriate binders/ books)
- Feeling disrespected by the teacher (being talked over, being moved away from peers, being addressed in a rude tone, etc.)
- Establishing a consistent sleep routine to support your student being awake and focused in class
- Anything your student specifically asks for your support in

While your student may be hesitant to role-play a conversation about managing their homework or feelings of being bullied, it is important that we help them begin to build confidence for hard conversations and help give some supportive language. If your student, even with the help of conversation starters (see page 75) or practice, still does not feel confident enough to act on their next steps alone, offer to simply be there with them. Allow your student to remain in the driver's seat. Attend the meeting or sit next to them while they write the email, yet act only as the sounding board and the person who provides a validating head nod or eye contact. A simple smile that translates to "I'm here, you can do this" can positively reinforce your child as they learn to navigate difficult and/or uncomfortable situations.

For other practices or frustrations that include more long-term goals or multiple steps, such as organization and planning, having frequent, nonthreatening check-ins will likely be more productive than adding fuel to their unorganized fire. Precorrection is far more supportive than redirection. I'd recommend developing a simple system that your student can both count on and plan around. Simple steps over a longer time frame often leads to more success. If your student struggles to manage their coursework, often leaving them annoyed at their teacher's lack of grace for late work, start small with writing down what they did each day in class. The next week, build on that small step, adding additional responsibilities such as current homework assignments, ultimately working your way up to "backward planning," managing their classwork with other school, community, and family commitments.

Of course, if your student specifically asks for your support, offer guidance and your physical presence while, as mentioned above, they take the lead. Slowly releasing responsibility while giving them the language and guidance in next steps, such as how to write an email asking for support after class or a practiced example in how to formally introduce themselves, all provides real-world skills that your student can lean on to support them in similar or larger tasks in the future.

Circumstances where you may want to consider handling the situation

While the ultimate goal is to provide our youth the opportunities to learn the skills necessary for success outside of high school and our homes, they are still our children. While physically our student may appear to be ready to take on the world, there are situations that warrant adult intervention. If choosing to handle the situation for your child, I encourage you to still provide opportunity for reflection so you and/or your student can arrive at an emotional baseline. This, of course, is much easier said than done, yet it provides an incredible opportunity for your student to learn how to handle their big feelings. Provide validating and affirming statements to acknowledge that you hear your student's concerns. Also, because it is your teen who will be directly impacted by your next steps, I encourage you to talk through the steps you plan to take and how you are going to take them, and then invite your student to come along. If you are calling your student's administrator about a recent bullying incident, for instance, allow your student to hear you advocating on their behalf.

Or perhaps you've noticed a decline in your child's grades and an increase in their evening screen time, which leads you to believe that they aren't getting enough sleep. Rather than imposing restrictions and having that be that, have a conversation.

But, while I am a huge advocate for involving your student in every process, I do believe that there are times when we need to make decisions that our children will not agree with. Evaluate, explain, and then execute. Even if you get it wrong, you can start back at the beginning; reevaluate, reexplain, and reexecute. There are no simple or perfect solutions for any situation. Talk through this process and acknowledge that, because we are dealing with real people and real feelings, we may not get it right the first time around—and that is okay. Here are some situations where adult intervention is needed:

- Cyberbullying or the distribution of videos or pictures of or by your student
- Violation(s) to your child's IEP or 504 plan
- Restricting technology (cell phone) use during classroom hours
- Arranging a mediation between your child and their teacher
- Any alleged racist, sexual, or illegal behavior from the teacher

From my experience as a high school educator, your student's teacher wants to build and maintain a positive relationship with each of their students. Moreover, the teacher also wants to have a positive working partnership with you. Never hesitate to reach out to an educator and ask about how the two of you, or others at the school, can work together to best support and serve your student. Ask yourself, "Is this something I'd hope the school would call me about?" If the answer is yes, go ahead and reach out to your child's teacher. If the answer is, "I think my kid can handle this," then talk with your teen and give them the skills to do so.

Closing Advice

As adults, we are balanced among learning to let go, needing to provide support, and knowing when to intervene. Usually, the situation, while it seems urgent—especially when approached from an emotionally driven perspective—is not, in fact, urgent. Take time to pause, step away, reflect, and revisit in order to assess the course of action that best fits your student in that situation, as well as figuring out your desired outcome. A well-thought-out course of action is more effective than a hasty response. Your student's frustration(s) with their teacher(s) is likely not the first or last time they'll experience these emotions. By navigating these situations intentionally, we can give our teens the life skills needed to engage with people they may not always agree with. You are giving your child the gift of problem-solving, as well as your partnership in managing the big stuff.

Conversation Starters

- How was your day at school? Did anything interesting or challenging happen?
- I noticed you seemed a bit [insert emotion: upset, quiet, etc.] after school. Do you want to talk about what happened?
- Was there a highlight or a not-so-great moment in your day?
- It is okay to have hard days and feel upset. How are you feeling about your school day?
- I received a call from your teacher today. Can you share your perspective on what happened?
- How did you feel during the situation that the teacher mentioned? Are you still feeling that way?
- What do you think led up to the incident the teacher described?
- Looking back, is there anything about the situation that you would handle differently?
- Is there something you wish your teacher understood better about you or the situation?
- How do you think the situation affected you and the other individuals involved?

Chapter 9
CONSTRUCTIVE PARENT-SCHOOL RELATIONSHIPS

How to keep it positive

Brian Skinner
2023 Kansas State Teacher of the Year

As educators, our jobs are to help each and every child so they are prepared to attain their own best success. We enter this profession because of our passion for teaching others, helping others, and building up the next generation. The public school system's model focuses on helping kids—period. In the same way, parents want to see their children grow up to achieve success, and every child hopes to be able to find a life path where they gain a sense of accomplishment. When looking at any form of parent and school relationship, it's important to remember that we all have the same goals.

Assuming Positive Intentions

In my experience as a public school educator, constructive relationships of any kind start with communication. So, before really considering how a constructive parent-school relationship can form, it is important to look at how individuals can ensure and maintain effective communication. Only then can the essential dialogue of helping a child succeed genuinely happen.

Early in my career, I attended Adaptive Schools Foundations Training through the Kansas State Department of Education. The focus was on collaboration and communication, and my biggest takeaway came from the norm of **assuming positive intentions**, remembering that all stakeholders in a child's education want the same result. Effective communication cannot happen if a party approaches situations with assumptions. And, while this may seem like a simple and obvious standard within communication, in my experience it is one of the first and easiest communication norms to drop away. For example, an accusatory email from a parent could read:

> "My child came home from school and told me that he was sent to the principal's office just because he was talking to his friends. Can you explain to me why you sent him out for such a small issue? He also said that everyone else was talking, too, and I would like to know what punishment you are giving everyone else."

This makes assumptions that the parent thinks their student recognized their behavior in the moment and that they also recognized what was happening around them and thought they were unfairly made an example of. It also makes the teacher feel like they need to be on the defensive, which harms productive dialogue and trust. Instead, the parent could provide better space for constructive dialogue by sending an email like this:

> "Good morning, I was hoping to touch base with you about my son and his day. He came home frustrated because he was sent to the principal's office during your class. I was hoping you could give me some more information as to what happened so I can help support both you and him going forward."

In this example, the parent gives space for the teacher to talk through their classroom setup, give context to a situation, and provide their perspective. Not only that, but they are also likely to feel freer to engage because of the difference in parental tone and intent. If parents and educators both assume positive intentions, there is stronger dialogue around the success of the student.

Front-Loading the Relationship

Too often within a parent-school relationship, the first communication takes place when there is a concern. And if there is never a concern, the first communication happens at parent-teacher conferences or sometimes never. This is a missed opportunity, and that's because of **relational capacity**, which is a measure of trust between two or more individuals. Within the school system, the ability for an individual to accept feedback from another is directly proportional to the relational capacity they have with the other individual. That is to say, if a parent, teacher, or student has not built a relationship with one of the other parties, it is impossible to effectively have an impact when giving either positive or negative feedback.

Trust doesn't come naturally, and there are little things that both the teacher and the parent can do at the start of each year to begin building it. For example, each educator has the opportunity to initiate contact early, with information about their course, a rundown of their processes, an introduction of themselves, or the methods to use to contact them with questions. Parents share this same opportunity. A simple note to introduce themselves or their child, explain how and when they can best be contacted, and what they hope to see for the year goes a long way in making visible a parent's active investment in their child's education.

Within the special education world, which is where I primarily teach, I have found that early engagement with parents has paid dividends for all. That initial conversation often turns into a discussion about a child's unique strengths and interests, as well as their deficits, and a better understanding why specific accommodations are in their individualized education plan (IEP). This conversation helps me differentiate my instruction to ensure I am aligning an objective appropriately for each child. And, although I am speaking of this primarily through the lens of a special education teacher, it is every bit as applicable for a general education student, because *all* students benefit from having instruction individualized for their learning needs.

Avoiding Unnecessary Conflict

Because educator, parent, and student should all have the same goal of seeing a student succeed, the question "Why is there conflict?" inevitably enters many people's thoughts. The conflict most often stems from a disconnect on *how* to reach that success. On one hand, there is a professional educator who has studied for years to understand pedagogy and child development and has spent sometimes decades honing their practice through experience. On the other hand, there is a parent who has spent more than a decade caring for their child, helping them grow up, and knowing them best. So, if the conflict over which voice is "most important" arises, I have provided a list of dos and don'ts from an educator's perspective that can help ensure both voices complement each other in the end.

DO: **Remember that the teacher has many students.** As educators, we balance many students, prepare for several different courses, and spend the majority of our contracted day teaching—therefore, we are not always at our computers or by our phones. This does not mean that any child is less important, but it does indicate that we may not have the ability to always act immediately.

DON'T: **Assume that if teachers don't respond immediately, they don't care.** Because we have so many duties assigned every day, it may take 24 hours for an initial acknowledgment response and potentially longer for a more detailed response.

DO: **Reach out to the teacher to ask for more information.** In a situation where a potential struggle exists, the teacher often knows additional information that is helpful to understanding the "why" behind a given event or procedure. There are district expectations, research-based best practices, and the need to balance an environment of 25 or more students. Each of these plays a role in why an educator does what they do.

DON'T: **Reach out to the teacher, assuming all parties already have all of the information.** It is important to listen to the student. However, even under the best of circumstances, misunderstandings and misinterpretations happen. Most conflict I observe stems from a student perceiving a situation one way, expressing it that way to a parent, and said parent sending an accusatory email. This stifles solutions, cuts off communication, and discounts the fact that there may be other factors in play that the student is not privy to.

DO: **Focus on the root of the struggle/conflict, as opposed to a symptom of the struggle.** We often get caught up in the symptom of a problem and only focus on that symptom, instead of its root. This is reactive and allows a struggle to continue. Focusing on the root cause of conflict allows for healthier and more sustainable solutions.

DON'T: **Expect that results have to be seen immediately.** Often, the best solutions have delayed results. It takes time to implement a solution, establish routine, and collect data on an effective change. Be patient, continue assuming positive intentions, and support your child, the teacher, and the process.

DO: **Look for consensus in a solution that is least restrictive.** Solutions, exceptions, and accommodations should be designed to interfere with a student's day as little as possible. This provides the opportunity for the student to adapt so they can potentially grow past the need for an accommodation. Allowing the solution to be least restrictive also allows for the least potential stigma for the teen.

DON'T: **Expect an all-or-nothing accommodation.** The end goal should be something workable, and that likely is not what was in any one individual's head from the start. The solution is built as a team and should be decided on through consensus, including the student's voice.

DO: **Include all relevant parties.** In many situations, several different team members should be involved. When trying to find the best solution, all relevant voices should be at the table.

DON'T: **CC higher-ups to make a statement.** Resolution should always happen at the lowest level possible. If a parent reaches out to a teacher with a concern and copies the principal, superintendent, or a state representative (yes, that happens), it presents a situation out of context and opens the possibility for uninformed and potentially unhelpful decisions. These messages typically result in more conflict, erode trust, and have a lack of resolution.

DO: **Engage consistently after the initial resolution.** Any solution, however well planned, might need adjustment. Consistent engagement keeps the dialogue going, the trust open, and the focus on the student's success.

DON'T: **Wait until another concern comes up to reach out to the teacher.** If the first follow-up arrives when there is another problem, that solution can be harder to reach than if dialogue had remained open throughout.

Meeting the Needs of Every Child

It is well-known that grades are important in high school. A grade of 60% or higher means a student passes a class, and achieving that consistently results in a diploma after their senior year. So yes, a child's grade is important, and because of its tie to a diploma, it often overshadows all else within a class. However, the grade should not be the focus, because the grade is a reflection of growth and skills learned. It's the skills and growth that are important. The question should not be, "How can my child's grade go up?" Instead, it should be, "What is causing my child's grade to be low?" to find the root of the problem.

- "She is frequently absent/tardy and therefore misses key instruction."
- "She rushes through assignments and struggles with accepting feedback to improve."
- "Poor time management and distractibility with peers result in missing or incomplete work."

These responses give more actionable ways to improve a grade, but, more importantly, focus on important skills that each child will need in their adult life. If a student passes a class but that grade does not reflect growth and skills learned, it means less—and when they graduate, their diploma will help them less. When everyone's focus is on the skills and growth, the grade will take care of itself.

It's important for both educators and parents to be aware of the pieces that can often interfere with growth mindsets and skills. I would put emphasis on three areas that can help a student focus on skills: consistency, technology/social media, and self-advocacy:

- **Consistency:** For any student, but especially those who are most prone to struggling, consistency is important; routines are important. Educators spend weeks at the start of every year establishing these routines. One of the best ways to support your student is to encourage routines and consistency at home. The duplication of routines outside school is important to reinforce the presence of routines at school.

- **Technology/Social Media:** Since the mid-2010s, technology and social media have become exponentially more important. It feels as though everything is instantly at our fingertips. As a result, there is a twofold problem. First, those skills/goals that require long-term investment are harder to obtain, because many have lost how to work toward a problem that takes time and dedication. And second, the cell phone can provide never-ending distractions, which comes with a need to be constantly engaged and a fear of being left out. Supporting technology-free time at home and social media boundaries allows for both improved attention span and focus and better social skills.

- **Self-Advocacy:** Most of our high school students are at an age where it is important for them to begin taking ownership of their work. When a student is struggling—although it is tough to witness—it's important to put the responsibility first on the teen and allow them to see how they can problem-solve. This teaches life skills and accountability. It's okay to experience struggle, because that allows for growth. NOTE: It is important, however, to be on the lookout for warning signs of larger concerns. Repeated negative patterns in the classroom, dramatic changes in social groups, consistent attachment to a cell phone, and sudden reclusive behavior are all signs that there may be a larger issue. In these situations, it is important to reach out to the teachers, administrators, and other support staff for direction and support.

Each of these three areas provides structure for a student so that school is an avenue toward learning, growth, and future success.

Closing Advice: We Are a Team

The 2023 Kansas Teacher of the Year team vision was "Education is what WE make it." We believe that everyone can achieve great things individually. But even more, we see that when we work as a team, we allow our strengths to align with each other, and that's where we make the biggest difference. Parents, students, and educators are teams, and we must function as a team, because when we do, we give each child their best chance at success. When we create open dialogue, struggles are more easily resolved. When we engage early and often, we foster trust. And when we keep the focus on what everyone's primary goal is—the success of each student—we lay the foundation that is needed for our school, community, and children.

Chapter 10
ONLINE CONNECTIONS

How technology affects your student in and out of school

Charlie McAdoo II, EdD
Career and Technical Educator, Georgia

As technology becomes a more prevalent part of our culture and society, students who come into learning environments will feel more inclined to use elements of it during instruction. Interactive web tools allow students to customize their learning experience and provide a social learning environment. However, the instruction must be designed in a manner that allows learners to share online resources, as well as collaborate. The instructional leaders should be responsible for coordinating, monitoring, and modeling the types of interactions they expect from learners. Parents should monitor and discuss online activity and student perspectives. These interactions give students a voice and choice in how they experience online environments. Students become accustomed to social interaction and digital collaboration and find online technologies to be a natural extension of their learning experience. Teachers, students, and parents should use technology to collaborate and promote learning inside and outside the classroom.

Technology Inside the Classroom

Implementing technology-oriented, project-based instruction is a transformative approach that immerses students in real-world scenarios, mirroring the current job market dynamics. This empowers students to authentically express themselves, fostering an environment where their creativity and skills can flourish. However, while encouraging this freedom, it is essential to establish guardrails within the learning experience.

These guardrails serve as guidelines, ensuring that students comprehend the tasks, assignments, and responsibilities. By delineating what is appropriate in both learning and workplace environments, these parameters provide students with a clear understanding of their boundaries, promoting a constructive and focused learning experience.

Furthermore, the involvement of parents in this process is crucial. Project-based instruction allows parents to play a pivotal role in their child's education. Parents can leverage this approach to instill a sense of accountability in their students, imparting valuable lessons on navigating and fulfilling roles in completing tasks, both large and small, within the online realm.

As technology continues to evolve, the importance of appropriate technology use becomes paramount. Teaching students how to use technology effectively and navigate the digital landscape responsibly is a vital aspect of their educational journey. With the right balance of freedom and guidance, technology-oriented, project-based instruction equips students with practical skills, instilling a sense of responsibility and preparing them for the demands of the modern workforce. It becomes a collaborative effort involving educators, students, and parents, shaping a generation that is tech-savvy, mindful, and accountable in their digital interactions.

Classroom Instructional Technologies

As technology advances, it becomes crucial for parents to comprehend the diverse tools employed by students and teachers inside and outside the classroom. Though your student may or may not proactively share information about the tools they use, be sure to engage in open and honest dialogue with them. These discussions should cover how your student interacts with their teachers, classmates, and others in physical and digital environments.

Unfortunately, a common misconception among students is that their online activities solely pertain to the digital realm. As mentioned, technology is increasingly integrated into daily life, evolving and shaping various aspects. Parents must recognize this reality and actively participate in discussions about their teenagers' online engagements—see the Conversation Starters at the end of this chapter for suggestions on how to spark these important interactions.

Listed below are some prevalent educational technology tools. The list is not meant to be exhaustive, as the technological landscape is dynamic and continually evolving. However, it aims to offer insight into some technologies your student may encounter during classroom instruction. This awareness lets you stay informed and engaged in your teen's educational journey in the digital age.

- **Online Learning Platforms.** High schools often use platforms like Google Classroom, Microsoft Teams, or learning management systems (LMS) for remote and blended learning.
- **Interactive Whiteboards.** Tools like SMART Boards allow interactive and collaborative learning experiences in the classroom.

- **Educational Apps.** Various apps cater to different subjects and skills, offering interactive learning experiences through tablets or smartphones.
- **Virtual Reality (VR) and Augmented Reality (AR).** Some high schools incorporate VR and AR technologies to provide immersive educational experiences, particularly in subjects like science and history.
- **Coding and Robotics Kits.** Schools may introduce coding and robotics kits to enhance students' skills in programming and problem-solving.
- **3D Printers.** High schools with STEM (Science, Technology, Engineering, and Mathematics) and art programs might use 3D printers for hands-on projects.
- **Collaboration Tools.** Platforms like Slack or Microsoft Teams are used for communication and collaboration among students and teachers.
- **Online Assessment Tools.** High schools may employ online platforms for quizzes, tests, and assessments to streamline the grading process.
- **Digital Textbooks.** Some schools have transitioned to digital textbooks, providing students with access to electronic versions of traditional textbooks.
- **Video Conferencing Tools.** Especially relevant for remote learning, video conferencing tools like Zoom and Microsoft Teams facilitate virtual classrooms and meetings.
- **AI-Based Educational Tools.** Artificial intelligence is becoming increasingly integrated into educational software to personalize learning experiences and provide targeted support.

Technology Outside the Classroom

Using technology in instructional environments opens up numerous possibilities for both students and parents, allowing them to extend the reach of classroom instruction. Beyond the confines of formal instruction, there's a vital aspect that parents should comprehend and actively engage with. Schools provide valuable tools for you to monitor your student's academic performance, and the consistent use of these resources, particularly parent portals, is highly encouraged.

Parent portals serve as comprehensive tracking systems, offering insight into your student's educational journey. From attendance records to classroom academic performance, standardized test scores, teacher comments, transcripts, and school district alerts, these portals provide a holistic view of your student's progress. I urge you to use these tools frequently for routine updates and as proactive measures to stay informed about your student's academic journey. By regularly accessing and monitoring information on parent portals, you contribute to a collaborative partnership with the school.

Importantly, this technological avenue becomes a crucial resource in emergencies or events demanding immediate parental attention. Keeping family information current ensures that the school and district have the necessary details to respond promptly to any unforeseen circumstances.

Equally significant is the awareness among students that their parents can monitor this information. This awareness instills a sense of shared responsibility for education and learning. Students comprehend that their educational journey receives support from the school, their parents, and, most significantly, from their own commitment to learning. This collaborative and informed approach enriches the educational experience, creating a supportive environment for students to thrive.

Parental Awareness

While technology offers numerous positive aspects that can contribute to your student's success both academically and in various aspects of life, it's crucial to remain mindful of the potential negative impacts, especially in the realm of social media. You should exercise vigilance to ensure your student's online safety. The following outlines key topics that every parent should be mindful of concerning teenagers and technology:

Privacy Settings

- Ensure that privacy settings are appropriately configured to protect personal information.
- Encourage teens to be selective about who can view their profiles and posts.

Cyberbullying

- Watch your teen for signs of cyberbullying, such as sudden changes in behavior, mood, or reluctance to use their devices.
- Encourage open communication about online interactions and peer relationships.

Online Predators

- Discuss the risks of interacting with strangers online.
- Emphasize the importance of not sharing personal information with unknown individuals.

Content Sharing

- Monitor the type of content your teen is sharing, including photos, videos, and personal details.
- Educate them about the potential long-term consequences of sharing inappropriate content.

Screen Time

- Set reasonable limits on screen time to ensure a healthy balance between online and offline activities.
- Be aware of signs of excessive use that might impact sleep, academic performance, or social interactions.

Digital Footprint

- Help your teen understand the concept of a digital footprint and the potential impact on future opportunities.
- Encourage responsible online behavior and the importance of a positive digital presence.

Inappropriate Content

- Use parental controls to restrict access to inappropriate or age-restricted content.
- Educate your teen about the risks associated with accessing or sharing explicit content.

Online Challenges and Trends

- Stay informed about current online challenges and trends to discuss potential risks and consequences.
- Encourage critical thinking and skepticism about participating in viral challenges.

Fake Profiles and Impersonation

- Teach your teen to recognize fake profiles and potential signs of impersonation.
- Advise against accepting friend requests or messages from unknown or suspicious accounts.

Mental Health

- Be alert to signs of mental health issues related to social media use, such as anxiety, depression, or low self-esteem.
- Encourage open conversations about the impact of social media on mental well-being.

Location Sharing

- Discuss the risks of sharing real-time location information and encourage responsible use of location-sharing features.
- Ensure that location settings are configured appropriately for safety.

Monitoring Apps

- Consider using monitoring apps to track online activity and set parental controls.
- Balance monitoring with trust-building and open communication.

Social Media Educational Resources

- Stay informed about social media platforms and their features.
- Use educational resources and online safety guides provided by platforms to enhance awareness.

Closing Advice

As you contemplate the role of technology in your student's life, it is essential to engage in open and honest conversations about its usage. Approaching these discussions should not adhere to a rigid "good or bad" binary. There are constructive ways to address technology without infringing upon your teen's dignity and individuality. For teenagers, technology serves as a platform for self-expression. While you may not always grasp the nuances of how your teen expresses themselves digitally, it's crucial to recognize that teens seek support, trust, and a sense of safety. To facilitate these essential dialogues about technology use, I recommend the following conversation starters.

Conversation Starters

- "Let's go over your social media privacy settings together. It's important to ensure your profiles are secure. Do you know how to manage them?"
- "Have you ever witnessed or experienced cyberbullying? I'm here to support you. Let's talk about how to handle such situations."
- "Online safety is crucial. Have you ever felt uncomfortable with someone online? Let's discuss ways to stay vigilant and protect yourself."
- "Let's talk about the content you share online. How do you decide what's appropriate? Establishing boundaries is important."

- "I've noticed your screen time has increased. Let's discuss healthy limits for device use and find a balance that works for you."
- "Have you thought about the long-term impact of your online presence? Let's discuss creating a positive digital footprint."
- "If you ever come across inappropriate content online, what would you do? Let's talk about strategies for handling such situations."
- "Fake profiles can be concerning. Have you encountered any? Let's discuss how to identify them and stay safe online."
- "How does social media affect your mood? It's essential to prioritize your mental well-being. Let's talk about your online experiences."
- "I noticed you share your location online. Let's discuss the pros and cons and set boundaries to ensure your safety."
- "Have you heard about monitoring apps? Let's discuss how they work and whether you're comfortable with the idea of using them."
- "Online grooming is a serious concern. Do you know what it is? Let's talk about recognizing and avoiding potentially harmful situations."

Chapter 11
FINDING PASSIONS IN AND OUT OF SCHOOL

How to support your student's interests

Jada Reeves
2019 West Virginia State Teacher of the Year

"Passion is energy. Feel the power that comes from focusing on what excites you." —Oprah Winfrey

Yes, we want our students to become responsible citizens with jobs and careers. However, it is also important that teenagers find something they enjoy doing that is not related to academics. Partaking in extracurricular activities and enjoying hobbies is important for a well-rounded individual who does not always focus on work. Ensuring that our teens find something they love to do and that excites them is the key to this chapter. Asking about "interests" or "curiosity" may help 15- and 16-year-olds understand what we want to understand.

The thing about passions, though, is that they change depending on your life stage. As adults, the same activity that interests us now may differ from what we were passionate about as a teenager or 10 years ago. A teenager may give you the customary response they give when you ask their opinion: "I don't know." Honestly, this answer is okay if it is the first time your child has been questioned about their passion. As a teenager myself, I would have probably said the same thing.

What is Passion?

Passion allows children to find themselves through self-discovery and reflection. Knowing one's purpose and passion also aids in exhibiting intrinsic motivation and setting goals. In life, we do not receive rewards as external motivation when completing a task, because enjoying the process is the key. Truly relishing an activity changes the perception between "having to" and "wanting to." The "wanting to" begins with finding that passion or interest and creating a purpose in life.

Sometimes you may wonder where your baby has gone and who the creature residing in your house is. But parenting teenagers, specifically 10th graders, can be gratifying once you find common ground. Teenagers are lovely illustrations of vivacity. Your child may test your patience while also making you realize their stubbornness will help them later in life. Tenth graders balance their independence and strength with needing you in their vulnerability.

Instead of using the phrases "finding your passion" or "what do you want to be when you graduate?", you should reword your questions to:

- Are there topics you like to find on TikTok or Instagram to watch?
- When you scroll through Instagram, what are some of the themes of the videos you view?
- Who do you follow on YouTube?
- What are some of the things you are curious about?
- What inspires you to change?
- Is there anything you like to participate in that excites you?

Our Role as Parents

As a parent of teenagers, a coach for athletes, and a teacher, my sole focus with children is for them to realize that we care and love them for who they are and who they are becoming. Parents should not focus on the world's external criteria or their own presumptions about their children. Focusing on praise and feedback for the child when they discover an interest should be geared toward the qualities the child possesses instead of their performance, so undue pressure is not evident. For example, if your child loves music and is extremely artistic, forcing your child to participate in a travel soccer team may be unwise unless they truly love it. Another example may be that you were the lead trumpet player in your school band, but your child does not have a musical bone in their body and instead loves to run. To encourage your child to continue violin lessons when they would rather be running cross-country would not make sense. Your child is not you, so focus on what they like and what they are interested in. If you do not take their interests into consideration, there will be a little extra pushback, eye rolls, some attitude, and resistance from your child. Extracurriculars should be fun and enjoyable for children!

You made these amazing humans and raised them for the last 15 years. However, they may not have the same interests, ideas, assumptions, or hobbies as you, which is okay. You may have heard of parents living their lives vicariously through their kids. I beg you not to do this. This is detrimental to the person they are becoming. One joy we have as parents is to love and enjoy our children and what makes them who they are. They should have the freedom to discover themselves with your direction and support. You have guided them this far; let them finish growing into their complete selves.

All people really need is to feel loved and accepted, especially teenagers. The concept of acceptance means that the child has a purpose in what they truly want out of their lives, not what their parents want them to do. Teenagers in 10th grade need to find themselves and enjoy their time in high school. These are the shaping years. What parent does not want their child to be happy? Support them for who they are and who they are becoming through your steadfast and unconditional love and acceptance.

Parenting can be hard. Your child is in high school and becoming an independent person who will eventually not need you every day. But your child *does* need you right now. They need you to help them make decisions, sort their thoughts, and support them. Allowing your child to choose which path to take helps shape who they will become and their ultimate purpose in life. Your child's successes and disappointments allow them to learn from the decisions they make and how to persist and persevere. Those learning experiences they encounter can lend themselves to passions and help them write the story of their lives with ideas they create through their interests and hobbies.

Experiences from Parents of 10th-Grade Students

I asked parents of current 10th-grade students what they have done to help their teens find the interests and activities they enjoy.

What have you tried to help your teen find a passion?

> "I present her with options on extracurricular activities and educational opportunities and give encouragement and positive reinforcement when something seems to spark interest." —Stacy C.

> "Encourage him to explore different things in life. I allow him to be bored and communicate with him what some of my passions were while growing up." —Christina C.

How do you support your child in finding a passion outside of school and academics?

> "Always being there, keeping a communicative relationship, and not letting their path offend me. I avoided receiving disinterest as unappreciative and taught my kids language to use. They learned to say, 'This isn't for me, but I enjoyed seeing the activity.'" —Allison S.

> "I try and remove any barriers that there might be for him to pursue something that interests him. He picked up a bass at a community program once, and then I happened upon a used bass and got it for him. He became a part of the church music team and was able to fine-tune his skills." —Matthew L.

> "As a parent, I feel it's important to participate with your child so they know their passion is valid. Being there and physically showing up is extremely important for a child mentally when supporting their passion." —Stacie H.

What is important in your family? How do you instill that in your child?

> "It is important that my kids find their role in the world. How can you find your true passion and not see and experience the world? We visit museums, sporting events, and community festivals and travel as much as possible. For me, budgeting our financial resources to prioritize experiences over material things has played a major role. I also have led by example and continue to follow my own passions while prioritizing time, encouraging their interests, and being an observer always in their journey toward being a passionate person." —Allison S.

> "Traveling and experiencing other cultures. We constantly encourage her in those areas and provide supplemental educational sources." —Stacy C.

"Hiking and camping are a big part of our family's dynamic. Hiking has always been a healthy outlet for us to unplug from technology and find healing and peace from being in the great outdoors. Some of the best conversations, breakthroughs, and dreams happen as we walk familiar and unfamiliar trails. Family hikes have always been mandatory. They are not always welcomed with enthusiasm but almost always end with gratitude and a stronger family bond." —Mason H.

How did you know when a hobby, sport, or activity was not working? What did you do to help your child decide what to do about it?

"We've tried many things over the years. With open communication, I've found that I just listen, and my kids have found their paths independently. My kids (almost all kids) seek acceptance from their peers and family members, and I focus on being the voice to continue to point the decision inward. I remind them this is their life and path, and they must make choices for themselves and avoid external sources of doubt and influence in their decision-making. I do want them to finish what they started. I want them to have a new activity they will try if they leave something." —Allison S.

"My son tried baseball and basketball before he found cross-country. When things got hard, we encouraged him to push through and not give up because it was difficult or not as fun as he thought it would be. Our only rule for quitting is that it has to be done after the end of a season because we always finish what we start. Often, he would give it another year and then decide it wasn't for him." —Taylor D.

Experiences from 10th-Grade Students

Next, I asked 10th-grade students in my school a series of similar questions.

What have your parents done to support you in finding a passion outside school and academics?

"Always encourage trying new things, full support, and listen to my ideas." —Jaiden D.

"They paid for a bass. They encouraged me to take lessons with a family member. Dad helps me to eat healthily and runs with me." —Katie F.

"My parents take me places and do things with me. Sometimes I like [the places], and sometimes I don't. I know I don't like museums and history like my mom [does]. It is good to try the activities to see if the activities we try fit me well, though." —Jacob R.

What is important in your family? How do your parents show this is important?

"Traveling. Mom loves to do it; I do, too. My mom shows it by prioritizing it over other things, like eating out." —Mason N.

"They go out of their way to attend mine and my sister's games. They show up for us." —Katie F.

"Knowing our feelings. I can talk to my mom and dad about things that make me happy or bother me, and they help me through it." —Jacob R.

How could a parent help you more with finding an interest or passion?

"Talk more about some plans for the future." —Jaiden D.

"Taking you to things you want to go to, like wrestling meets or games." —Jacob R.

How could a teacher help support you with a passion or your interests?

"Give recommendations for outside activities. Be more involved with what students like and dislike." —Jaiden D.

"They could try to relate more. They could build a relationship with me to get to know me better. They could introduce more interesting ideas." —Katie F.

"Look at how I act and what I do in class and find something that fits that student. The adult could seem excited when you talk about it to them." —Mason N.

Advice from Current 10th-Grade Extracurricular Coaches and Leaders

The following are questions I shared with other coaches in West Virginia and their responses and advice.

What have you tried to do to help your student or athlete find a passion?

"In 10th grade, some students are just entering high school and have never tried certain activities. If I see a student in the hallways during school hours, I try to recruit them to come to the wrestling room or come to workouts for football. They do not like what they have yet to attempt, so encouraging students to get involved is important." —Coach Randall P.

"Realize each child will come to you and need different things from you. Some teenagers need you to talk to them, some need encouragement, and some need you to listen. Be aware of what they need at the time, and be flexible with your expectations. Teenagers' brains have not developed yet, so the adult in their life, whether a parent or coach, needs to support the child in what they need at that particular moment." —Coach Jeremy R.

What advice do you have for parents to support their child in finding a passion or interest?

"First, show your child that you care. Talk to them about their friends, progress in school, life plans, or even what shows and movies they like. When you show up, kids know that. Letting your child know that you want them to find things they like to do is important and that you will support them no matter what." —Coach Squire W.

"Listen. That is all you need to do sometimes. Listen to what your child is telling you and support them." —Coach Jerry B.

"Be patient. Kids are still trying to discover themselves—let them. That is how they become an individual." —Coach Jeremy R.

Closing Advice

As someone who advocates for children to find what they love to do and pursue it, I applaud you for reading this chapter. You may hear those grumbles and complaints and possibly get an eye roll. However, I assure you that your child will look back on this year and appreciate all you have done to help them through 10th grade. Giving your teen the knowledge that you are invested in their happiness, no matter what it is, demonstrates love, patience, and acceptance.

Although we want our students to plan ahead for their lives after graduation, finding interests may assist them in associating their passion with a possible career. Remember, we are raising our children to thrive and flourish for the rest of their lives. I am excited for your family to embark together and discover your child's interests and passions this year!

Chapter 12
FINDING PASSION IN SPORT

How to support your high school athlete

Sara Skretta, EdD, PHR
2003 Nebraska Assistant Principal of the Year

Navigating the myriad interests and aspirations as a teenager can be both thrilling and daunting. As 10th graders stand at a point of self-discovery, the search for passion becomes an important piece of the journey to shape their character and influence their future. Sports are central to many sophomores, a source of physical fitness and a powerful opportunity for personal growth and fulfillment in the crazy world of 10th grade.

Sports present an ideal platform for teens to express themselves beyond textbooks and classrooms. The playing field or court becomes a place where they can live out their dreams and unique personalities. The potential impact sports can have on fostering a sense of purpose extends far beyond the field of play for both students who are academically inclined and those who are less so.

Because I am an educator, my four sons should have been dedicated to academics, right? Well, they were, but what I realized is that their definition of "dedication" to academics was not only different from mine, but different from each other's as well. The key is to support each child based on individuality.

Life Skills and Well-Being

I am an enthusiastic supporter of involvement in school sports and activities. The engagement with school that 10th graders have by participating in sports is powerful for overall high school success. They learn to build relationships with other students and coaches, shape focused motivation to perform as an individual and a member of a team, and develop the emotional tools to handle elation, dejection, anger, frustration, and happiness—all things that are invaluable life skills. Knowing there are people counting on them and that they need to be prepared, present, and give 100% are also useful skills for the rest of their lives.

It's also important to monitor your sophomore's physical well-being. An athlete needs proper nutrition, enough sleep, and rest days to prevent injuries. These things are equally essential for your 10th grader as a student and a human being. Not that this is easy, as I experienced when my son was trying to build muscle. He knew he needed protein, but he only ate strawberries and chicken and, seemingly overnight, his weight had drastically dropped. We had a conversation about his goal and helped him with his meal planning to meet it in a healthy way.

During 10th grade, athletes begin to differentiate themselves—those who are competing for or have secured a varsity position, those who aren't there yet, and those who may just play recreational or intramural sports. It is important to help balance the requirements and dedication or self-motivation by students to their sport with the academic requirements to remain eligible. While the coaches may have run these by their student-athletes, parents can also locate the academic requirements in the school's student handbook or by contacting the athletic department.

This is the year to have a conversation with your 10th grader to gauge their interest in playing sports in college. Even if you don't think your student has what it takes, development can often accelerate during 10th grade, so supporting your teen and keeping options open is important.

College Sports

Your sophomore should understand what is involved in being a collegiate athlete, as well as the steps required to get there. If your student has expressed an interest in playing at the next level, I highly recommend having them meet with their high school counselor to learn about academic eligibility requirements, deadlines, what the NCAA Eligibility Center entails, and other processes. Access the NCAA Eligibility Center website for information on helping your student-athlete. This will help you guide your teen, even if you are new to the idea of collegiate sports.

Your athlete should communicate with coaches their desire to play at the next level. Coaches are frequently contacted by collegiate coaches and can promote your athlete, as well as provide recommendations if they know your athlete wants to pursue sports in college. Keep in mind that some coaches are more well-connected and experienced with collegiate athletics than others. It is also important that your teen find ways to showcase their athletic ability, whether that be at camps, through invite-only opportunities, or on social media.

I would strongly encourage you to find a parent who has recently managed the recruiting process, as it can be overwhelming. Knowing how someone else navigated this journey is very helpful. A word of caution: The recruiting process can become addicting for both students and parents and can easily become your only focus. It is imperative that you help your 10th-grade athlete manage expectations, as chances are greater they will *not* play beyond high school than that they will. In fact, the NCAA estimates that only 7.3% of high school football players, as an example, will play in any of the three collegiate divisions, I, II, or III. (Go to ncaa.org to see the full list of sports.)

It is not an easy discussion, but when talking to your teen about the realities of collegiate athletics, it is critical you do so in a supportive way. Ask your student if they want to just *play* the sport or if they want to play the sport at a certain level (i.e., NCAA Division I). If your athlete simply wants to keep playing, that opens up many more opportunities at all levels of college athletics. If your athlete specifies a certain level, like NCAA Division I, be supportive but transparent about the realities, like sharing the fact that most high school athletes won't make it to that level and, if they do, only a small percentage play. Helping your teen understand the difference between the dream and the reality at the beginning of their high school sports journey will make your recruiting process smoother.

Academics

While teenagers are in-season, support them athletically *and* academically to assist in their overall personal development. During 10th grade, students should begin to become their own advocates at school, know the academic responsibilities and requirements to maintain athletic eligibility, and understand how their high school classroom and overall performance could affect recruitment if they've chosen to pursue that path.

Sophomores who want to devote significant energy and time to prepare for athletic competition versus academics may require more frequent parental support and intervention. Have a conversation with your student that clearly outlines your expectations for their academic performance in-season and during the off-season. We were very direct with our sons before their 10th-grade sports seasons began: They must not get behind in school and they needed to, at a minimum, meet the school's eligibility requirements for GPA. We purposely did not demand a specific GPA or grade in a particular class, as we had four different learners with four very different opinions of their school experience, but we were specific about the social consequences that would occur if these expectations were not met. Being direct like this reinforces to your 10th grader that the knowledge and study skills acquired in the classroom are just as, or more, important as the physical skills they gain on the field/court.

Academic achievement, whatever that looks like for your student, is important. As parents, however, we need to be prepared to let go of our own ideas about our child's abilities on the field or court, in the classroom, and/or in concurrently managing these things as a 10th grader. A student simply may not have the bandwidth or physical ability to execute at a high level academically during their sport's season. While it is important to outline your expectations, you should be flexible within those expectations to support your athlete. This should not be confused with lowering standards, but rather navigating different roads at different times. For example, one of my sons performed extremely well academically during football season because he loved his sport and coach. He did not want to disappoint the expectations the coach shared, was very organized because he had little unscheduled time, and he used his time wisely. Once the season ended, it was like pulling teeth to get that same performance because his motivation decreased!

School Engagement and Socializing

Many 10th-grade athletes dream of playing at the college level but derive even greater value from the friendships, self-worth, personal satisfaction, and enjoyment they get from their sport. I can't emphasize enough the value sports bring during 10th grade related to school engagement, leadership and teamwork skills, self-motivation, and self-regulation skills, especially related to the final years in high school.

To parent a 10th-grade student-athlete is to be aware that not only are they involved in sports because they love the competition or because their friends are on the team, but because they are also fully engaged as a high school student. To avoid sports taking over, encourage a variety of interests. Even the most gifted athlete may not extend their playing time beyond high school, so having other interests helps develop a more well-rounded individual, prevent burnout, and expand options for downtime.

High school is a time for socialization within, and outside of, a team. This provides 10th graders the opportunity to develop personal skills and navigate social situations. However, it is important to discuss social boundaries related to sports eligibility. Discuss possible consequences for various social choices, and equip your 10th grader with specific strategies to manage those situations. For example, if your teen is hanging out at a friend's house and someone brings beer, they will need to decide whether to drink a beer or leave. Student-athletes caught in this situation are often subject to a season suspension, even if they report the incident. We gave our teens the words to use in such a situation: "It's been great hanging out, but I need to go" or "Hey guys, I'm in season so I'm going to take off." Many 10th graders can't drive, so we made sure our sons knew that they just needed to text or call and we'd come pick them up.

We also talked with our teens about social media posting, texting, and possible ramifications for athletic participation. We told them that if they wouldn't show their grandmother the post then they should not be putting it out there for the rest of the world. Sending or receiving provocative or nude pictures can have legal and other ramifications for athletic participation, so specifically telling your teen how to deal with these issues is critical. Arming them with information can help them avoid making choices that could negatively affect athletic eligibility (and college eligibility in general!).

Communication

Open communication with a high schooler can be challenging, but maintaining it is essential. Be supportive and a good listener about their sport, but avoid providing additional coaching or sharing disappointment in your student's performance. Student-athletes have a tendency to shut down and share less if they think they will disappoint a parent or will be yelled at for their individual performance. Celebrating victories and achievements is important, but don't put too much emphasis on the wins or losses. Don't forget to also ask about school, friends, and other non-sports interests, too!

I found that the most challenging thing for a parent of a high school athlete is to respect their choices, as their interests often change and evolve. As a 10th grader, my son decided to stop playing basketball. It wasn't because he didn't like basketball, but he realized that due to his height (or lack thereof!), he had little to no chance of seeing the court and decided to focus on the other sports with which he felt he was having success. It was difficult to see him stop playing a sport he liked, but it was his decision, and I honored that. My role was to be open and approachable when he was making the decision and support him without judgment.

Time Management

Setting realistic expectations is important to help your teen understand that enjoying their sport and learning valuable life skills are equally important. Supporting balance will ensure that your sophomore's schedule includes time for academics, socializing, family, and sometimes just hanging out. Help your student balance their time to prevent overcommitment to a singular sport, even if they are a one-sport athlete. This balance requires careful planning, time management, and a commitment to maintaining well-being. Help your 10th-grade athlete allocate time for both academic and sports commitments using tools such as calendar apps or lists to organize their time.

Routines create a consistent sense of structure to make time for studying, practice schedules, and social activities. Two of our sons loved school and were able to maintain a high GPA all year long, including during the hockey season. They did not need much guidance to find time to study or complete homework and demonstrated a good balance between sport and school. Another son loved football more than he loved school, and it was his preference to watch film or nap instead of doing homework. He was meeting eligibility requirements during the season but, toward the end of the season, when he was also physically exhausted, we had to clearly provide him with structure at home to finish his academics before he moved on to other things to help him keep the privilege of participating in sports. Setting realistic expectations based on both academic and athletic ability is key to understanding each child.

Creating downtime and using it wisely can keep your 10th-grade athlete on track. Encourage the use of downtime between classes or on bus rides to games to review notes or complete assignments. Keeping study materials with them will make it easier to access when the opportunity presents itself. Or use downtime for doing nothing, gaming with friends, napping, or watching TV. Everyone needs to decompress, and I discovered I needed to help my 10th grader create opportunities for downtime and encourage him to "do nothing." On a weekend afternoon, for example, when there is nothing scheduled, encourage your teen to read a book for fun, go with you to the grocery store, or watch a movie.

Closing Advice

Sports transcend the boundaries of physical activity, becoming the way in which 10th graders can enhance their health and cultivate life skills, build resilience and confidence, and forge lasting connections. If your 10th grader chooses sports as their passion, you must be ready to guide and support them through the challenges of athletic competition, future athletic aspirations, academic balance, and managing social interactions. Sophomore year of high school is intense and critical to your child's development as a student, athlete, and person, and they need you more than ever this year.

> ### Conversation Starters
>
> - What are you learning in school this week?
> - What are your goals for this season and how can I help support you in achieving them?
> - How are you managing your time between homework and practice? How can I help support you in balancing this?
> - Is there anything challenging you right now with the team/coach and how can I help?
> - I'm so proud of the effort you're putting into both school and sports. What can I do to help make it even better?

Chapter 13
FINDING PASSION IN THE ARTS

How to support your high school artist

Sheena Graham
2019 Connecticut State Teacher of the Year

One day in class I said, "Please take out your choir folders." Everyone did except for one 10th grader named Tiffany, who immediately burst into tears. She and her mom had argued that morning before school and it was her birthday! Her response triggered something in other students, who began unburdening themselves of everything they were concerned about in their lives—being too fat, too thin, too dumb, too smart, too light, too dark, too tall, too short…and the bottom line? They could not seem to please anyone!

The following lyrics from my song, "Reaching Isn't Always Easy," describe their emotional state at that time:

> "There are days when I'm so lonely, days I feel so cold.
> Everything I reach for, I'm too young or too old.
> Too young to understand, too old to recognize.
> Too young to feel real love, too old real tears to cry." (lines 1–4)

"There are times when life seems heavy, and the road just seems too long.
You smile, you call me baby, but for hugs I'm too grown.
Too grown to need attention, too young to make my rules,
Too grown to need directions, too young to lose my cool."
(lines 10–13)

In my close to four decades as a performing arts educator, I have found that 10th graders, while in the process of becoming more independent and self-aware, are caught between childhood and adulthood. These students really need and value the support of their parents and/or guardians in ways that they often do not verbalize.

I often say, "It is the ink flowing from the pen that rescues me again and again." Tenth graders are at an important crossroads in deciding how their passion for the arts will play out in their future lives. Will it simply be an outlet for their emotions, or do they have the desire and drive to develop their strength in the arts into a career?

How to Support Your Teen's Interests in the Fine Arts and/or Performance

1. **Inquire about what your teen is working on.** Do not wait for them to ask for your support. Ask for their course calendar and integrate it into your own. Make a point to see/hear their works in progress. Based on your schedule and your teen's, decide on a check-in commitment that is reasonable (i.e., weekly, bimonthly, monthly), and then stick to it. This will allow you the opportunity to note and support their growth. In the process, you will also be encouraging your student to practice their art form.

2. **Provide a suitable place and a designated time for your child to practice.** For example, if your student is a dancer, that

means enough room for them to move around unimpeded. A visual arts student may require a room that has natural light. An instrumental or voice student needs a place where they can practice, with good acoustics and without their sound disturbing others.
3. **Create a supply/maintenance list.** Ask your teen what they need to develop their art form. They may have a list from their instructor. If so, make a copy of it. What is needed? When? Which items are a one-time purchase and which will need to be replaced weekly, monthly, or quarterly? Discuss how much advance notice is necessary for you to provide the needed maintenance of their instrument or purchase of supplies. They will need to develop this process as they move forward in the arts.
4. **Attend school conferences and do not skip meetings with the arts instructor(s).** The valuable information received from their arts educators will give you deeper insight into their strengths and weaknesses. These teachers will help you to understand the challenges that lie ahead, both in their current class and future courses. The educators can offer suggestions on how to address successes and failures and be able to list possible careers related to your child's abilities. This information will allow you to support your child in a more informed way.
5. **Help your teen decipher whether their art form is for love or career.** Do they create just because they love to do it, or is it something that they could see themselves making a career out of?
6. **Understand that a larger investment may be required.** Your child may require art supplies or an instrument of a higher quality, especially if they are considering the arts as a future career or source of supplemental income. Visual arts students will need to transition from beginner supplies to higher-quality brushes, pencils, erasers, measuring tools, clay, sketchbooks,

watercolors, acrylic paint, cameras, chalk, and canvas. The area of visual arts your teen is pursuing will decide their specific tools, including digital ones. Better equipment will allow for more precise and vibrant art. An instrumental student will need to transition to a higher-quality instrument. Depending on your budget, you may want to consider trade-in options or purchasing a refurbished instrument; your student's music teacher can help guide you.
7. **Attend live performances and exhibits together.** This is a motivating and inspirational way to help your teen grow artistically.
8. **Attend their performances/exhibitions and celebrate their successes.** Showing you care about them, and what matters to them, is the most important tip, and it goes a long way in boosting their confidence and belief in themselves. It also helps them to hold on through the moments when they suffer setbacks.

What Is Needed to Excel in the Field?

For an individual to excel in the arts, practice combined with drive, determination, and discipline are major steps in the right direction. Ask your child to meet with their school counselor to set goals for the school year and a timetable to review their progress toward reaching them. Your teen should explore the many career options that exist in the arts for those with their strengths and talents. Opportunities may be a little overwhelming initially. Don't be discouraged. Consider the strengths your child has beyond the arts, and see if that helps to slim the possibilities down a bit. For example, if your child is a strong musician and loves science and human anatomy, maybe music therapy is an option. A student who loves the arts and history might create pieces related to history, manage a museum, or curate collections. A child who is passionate about the arts and loves business could become an agent for artists or someone who creates opportunities for other artists.

Once your student has narrowed the list of careers down to three or fewer, it is time to review the coursework necessary to move forward. There is a good chance that there will be some overlap. Your teen should take those courses first. For example, piano might be required if they want to be an instrumental performer, a composer, a music conductor, or a voice major. School counselors are an excellent resource for identifying the courses students will need to pursue the careers they are interested in. However, parents and students can also find this information online by looking at application and audition requirements for colleges the student is considering. Searching online for the course requirements for their desired career is also an option. The National Association of Schools of Music (NASM) (nasm.arts-accredit.org/students-parents) is a great resource also.

If you come across requirements for classes not offered at your student's school, consider that nearby schools may offer the required course(s). Internships or apprenticeships may be available to help a student meet requirements. Your high school may even grant an independent study period to complete the necessary work. If offered, that is an opportunity you don't want to miss!

Take Advantage of Opportunities In and Out of School

School exhibits and performances are nonnegotiable—if they are offered at your school, your student should be participating. Yet it is vital to take advantage of opportunities outside of school also. The more exposure your child has while in 10th grade, the easier it will be for them to discover their future. Consider:

- What kind of commitment will be required for individual practice time versus group rehearsals, performances, and/or exhibit time?

- How much time will be required to get the materials needed to pursue your child's passion? Are they available locally? If so, how far away from your home or workplace are they? What are the store's hours? If the materials are available online, what is the difference in price?
- Are you able to support your teen's goals financially, or will you need to seek assistance? What are the requirements for financial aid? Is there financial support available through your local church? Does your workplace offer assistance? Are there scholarships available? Your teen's arts educator will be a good resource for what is available in your area.
- Will transportation be necessary—bus, train, rideshare? Are student passes or student discounts available? Or is the opportunity within walking or biking distance?

How well is your student doing academically? Are they maintaining their current responsibilities in other classes while excelling in the arts? If by some chance their grades start to drop, have you had a discussion about what needs to happen for your child to rebound? Are you prepared to implement those consequences?

For programs offered outside school, have you thought about which type will best support your child and their learning style? Is there an opportunity for private lessons that you can take advantage of? Have you discussed with your student's educators where support may be most needed?

Competitions and local contests expose your student to other artists in their age range. Summer programs do also. Art camps are beneficial, whether your child is a participant or mentoring younger students. I did not realize it at the time, but I believe that being a camp counselor planted the seed for my becoming a teacher; seeing the difference that support and a listening ear made with the children at camp impacted my life greatly.

Bring in Your Experience

Frequent conversations with your teen are helpful. Be willing to share your own experiences with the arts. I did not know until after my father passed away that he had been a guitarist. I never saw him touch a guitar, though I would hear him sing when he thought no one was listening. My dad had an amazing voice. I would have loved to talk music with him.

Have you ever taken any arts courses? If so, how did the classes make you feel? What courses do you have in common? What did you struggle with and how did you overcome the difficulty? If you did not take any arts classes, why not? Was it not an option? Was it due to finances? Answers to any of these questions will open the eyes of your teen to a part of you they don't know. Having you express your feelings may free them up to verbalize theirs. These conversations will open the door to other conversations.

Closing Advice

Reminding your 10th grader that you care about them by listening and having discussions will help keep them on track. Tiffany was one of many students in the classroom who went into the studio and recorded the song "Reaching Isn't Always Easy." These students also brought in pictures to make a video that became a tool I used to open my classes every school year. It allowed for discussions regarding expectations, current and future challenges, and the consequences of choices we make daily.

The passion of my students involved could not be denied, both in the group who did the recording and those who listened to it. And they are constantly evolving, like all 10th graders. Every day is not going to be filled with sunshine. But with your support and involvement they will realize:

"You reach on (though inside your heart is breaking)
You reach on (though you know that it's a risk you're taking)
You reach on (getting stronger with each step you're making)
You reach on, reach on…." (lines 19–22)

"Reaching isn't always easy, sometimes it's really hard.
Till you look back and realize just where you really are.
And you know you didn't do it, you've been guided all along
By the spirit of your loved one, by the spirit of their song
So you'll reach on…." (lines 5–8)

> ### Conversation Starters
>
> - How do you feel your latest performance/exhibit differed from your previous one?
> - What were you most excited about? Concerned about?
> - What arts classes do you feel challenge you the most and how?
> - If you could go to your dream art school, which one would it be and why?
> - What is your dream job?

Chapter 14

IS MY STUDENT READY FOR 11TH GRADE?

Advice from an 11th-grade teacher (and parent also in the trenches of the high school years)

Amybeth Taylor
English Teacher, New Hampshire

"I survived 10th grade!" reverberates within many parents' and caregivers' minds, rejoicing at the end of what may have felt like 7th grade all over again. While 10th graders are more mature than their 12-year-old selves, they can be just as misunderstood. We must remember why the term *sophomore* is historically assigned to 10th grade, and those sophomoric tendencies that we observe in our 15- and 16-year-olds are to be expected as they struggle to realize their place in the hierarchy of high school. Simply put, it's an awkward year for many teenagers.

Watching both my son, now a sophomore in college, and my daughter, now a junior in high school, stumble through 10th grade was heartbreaking and frustrating at times. While no parent likes to fall into the trap of wishing away time, 10th grade was a tough year to watch from the parenting sidelines, and I was relieved when June arrived with the promise of a summer break—time to recharge and reset.

Eleventh grade was looming, and I remember falling victim to the pressures associated with the reputation that junior year holds—the most difficult year of high school and the most important, in that it is the last full year before students traditionally apply to college. I wanted my own kids to feel ready for this pivotal year, and I had to keep myself in check to allow them to feel supported, not controlled. Questions like *What if they didn't keep up their GPA? What if they didn't take enough honors and AP classes? What if they can't handle the workload associated with their challenging classes?* are natural stressors for both parents and students.

How do we know that 10th graders are ready to meet those greater demands that actually *do* accompany 11th grade, and how can students feel supported and confident as they make the transition to the final years of high school?

I have taught secondary English for 15 years, with the most years spent working with 11th graders. When asked what I love most about teaching 11th-grade English, my response is the age and stage of the people I get to work with. Students emerge from 10th grade with a new sense of self and a new sense of purpose. For some, purpose derives from the fact that college is looming, while for others it is the relief that they are one year closer to graduation. For most students of this age, however, it is just as much about their new social status in the high school hierarchy, providing a confidence boost to accompany their growing intellectual curiosity and capability. Eleventh graders deepen their ability to apply analysis to not only their academics, but also to the world around them, making connections between learned knowledge and practical application. It really is a fascinating shift between the first and second half of high school.

My students begin the year with an extensive unit in narrative writing, with a focus on memoir. One of their favorite mini-projects is creating a symbolic "baseball mitt" on which they write favorite quotes, song lyrics, lines of poetry, or words of wisdom learned from those with more life experience. A handful of mitts are always inscribed with Babe Ruth's iconic line: "Never let the fear of striking out keep you from playing the game." This quote makes me smile, because it is heartwarming to know that 16-year-olds value struggle and failure as an important part of growth. And it also reminds me that they need to hear "You've got this!" often.

How to Help Teenagers Find Their People, Place, and Purpose

Level Up When Possible

While class schedules are generally finalized during the summer months, remind your student that there is an add/drop period at the start of the school year. If there is an opportunity to strategically add rigor to their schedule, suggest that your student try to level up when possible. For students who have mostly completed college prep-level courses, this is a good opportunity to explore an honors-level course or two, especially in those academic subjects that are most interesting or that might support future academic or career plans. And this is an important year for Advanced Placement and dual-enrollment opportunities that might help students earn college credits while still enrolled in high school.

It can be easy to miss opportunities for academic challenge if a student has been taking courses consistently at one level. Teachers and counselors are receptive to conversations with students and their parents, and it is gratifying for all involved to see students challenge themselves, so set up a call or a meeting to discuss current progress and future placement to ensure appropriate rigor and future preparation. Make sure that your student is not delaying important coursework that should be completed during their junior year. Doing so will add additional stress to senior year. Basically, this is a good time to do a course and credit audit with your student and their counselor.

My 11th graders acknowledge that it is a good idea to balance the workload with some hard and some easier classes. In addition, consider whether a study hall might be a good idea to provide focused work time during the school day, especially for those students with busy extracurricular schedules.

A Sense of Purpose

Finding ways to highlight and build upon past successes boosts self-efficacy and positivity about the future. Empower your new 11th grader with reassurance in order to cultivate their growing need for independence and to allow them the chance to find their purpose. It amazes me how many 11th graders write about the idea of purpose and belonging in their writer's notebooks, narratives, and poetry. They thrive on human connection and shared purpose.

If a rising 11th grader is struggling to find purpose in academics, sports, clubs, friendships, or part-time employment, this is a prime time for a little supportive nudging from trusted adults.

Students who attend the first day of an athletic tryout or the first club meeting of the year feel a more comfortable sense of belonging right away. Many high schools offer club fairs within the first weeks of school. Encourage your child to attend and sign up for one or two activities that seem interesting. Students who get involved in their school community in some way tend to feel a deeper sense of belonging and connection to their peers. Plus, this builds positive relationships with the teacher who supervises the club or activity.

Establish Relationships

Peer relationships are essential, but so is the need to establish respectful relationships with teachers from whom a student might ask for letters of recommendation. By the time senior year rolls around and a student is applying to colleges or for scholarships, internship opportunities, or employment, they will appreciate the relationships they formed with teachers during junior year. I tell my students this early on in the year, reminding them they will most likely seek out recommendations from their 11th-grade teachers, who have the most recent knowledge of their strengths. It is important to remember the old adage—first impressions are lasting impressions. Encourage your new 11th grader to start the year off on a positive note, keeping in mind how they want to be regarded by their teachers and peers. Each year truly is an opportunity for a fresh start!

Communication Skills

The summer between 10th and 11th grade is a good time to remind teenagers of the importance of their online presence, specifically a presence that they know will represent their best self. If they haven't done so already, teenagers should establish routines around checking school email regularly. If a personal email account has not yet been established, help your student set one up using an appropriate account name. This will be especially important as students correspond with potential employers and colleges in the coming year or two.

It's also essential that students are aware of proper etiquette around emailing teachers with questions about assignments or grades:

1. Acknowledging the issue
2. Explaining their desired outcome
3. Proposing a solution that keeps their own responsibility at the forefront of the correspondence
4. Thanking them for their time

If your teenager hasn't yet developed the habit of emailing teachers when absent, now is the time to start.

College Discussions, Future Planning, and Standardized Testing Preparation

October is PSAT month for many juniors. This test is not only preparation for the spring SAT, but it also presents scholarship opportunities for high-achieving students. The summer before 11th grade can be a good time to investigate this and any other standardized tests offered by your student's school. Some schools offer the PSAT to 10th graders. If your student has already taken the PSAT, reviewing their scores together can be informative. If there is one area in which your student struggles, reach out to the testing coordinator or a guidance counselor at school. There are plenty of test prep tools that can help.

Teenagers are very grounded in the here and now, while we parents typically project out a year or two, thinking about where our children might be after graduation. Helping our teenagers appreciate the impact of their current choices on their future accomplishments can be a feat! The simple act of acknowledging that we appreciate the challenges they face as they think about their future can be profound in the teen-adult relationship.

Boundaries, Limits, and Time Management

Balancing academics, extracurricular activities, part-time employment, family time, and a social life presents a challenge for many teenagers. Eleventh graders sometimes need to know that it's okay to establish boundaries around their time and priorities. How can you help your teen to navigate this balance? Hold them to high standards and expectations, while also being understanding and supportive of the many demands on their time by offering constructive solutions.

Each week, I ask my students to map out their week like a stove by thinking about burners on high, medium, low, and simmer. It's impossible to attend to multiple responsibilities all set over a high flame. Something will inevitably burn. Prioritizing coursework and a manageable number of extracurricular activities is essential. I like to think of the last two years of high school as training for the expectations of college or the workforce. Discussions around time management, healthy sleep and eating habits, and attention to well-being are important before starting a new school year.

Closing Advice

- Empower and cultivate independence in your new 11th grader by encouraging them to take more responsibility for initiating conversations with teachers, as well as taking advantage of opportunities to become part of the school community.

- Set up a course and credit audit with your student and their academic counselor to make sure they are registered for classes that offer the right level of challenge and that best support their future plans and goals.

- Remind your child of the importance of time management and the need to balance priorities. The stovetop analogy of burners on high, medium, low, and simmer works well with teens. *I can't do everything, but today I can _____ is another way in which I ask my students, as well as my own children, to set priorities to minimize the stress associated with more demanding academic expectations.

- Responsible and respectable online presence reminders are helpful at any stage in a teenager's development, and it is extremely important in the last years of high school. Teenagers want to represent their best selves!

- Appropriate communication skills are a must. This includes the ability to email teachers when absent or with questions, check their emails on a daily basis, and to know how and where they can find their class assignments from day one of the new school year.

Your teen appreciates that you care and want to be involved in their education, and they benefit from the acknowledgement that you understand they are about to embark on a pivotal year of high school. Teenagers may act annoyed by our questions, but they ultimately appreciate the interest.

Conversation Starters

- Reflecting back on 10th grade, what accomplishments are you proud of?
- What was one of your biggest challenges during 10th grade?
- What sorts of tools or strategies have you developed to handle challenges more constructively?
- Is there anything that your 11th-grade teachers should know about you?
- If so, do you feel comfortable sending them an email before school starts, introducing yourself and telling them who you are as a learner and as a person?
- What extracurricular activities do you plan to get involved in this year? Where can you find out about school clubs and organizations?
- Which classes are you most looking forward to in 11th grade?
- Do you feel that appropriate class levels—CP, honors, AP, dual-enrollment —are reflected in your schedule?
- What are some of your concerns about starting 11th grade?
- What can you do during the summer months to feel more prepared for 11th grade? Are there summer assignments for classes to complete? Are there special materials that you know you'll need for your new classes?
- Is there a trusted adult at school who you can count on for support when needed?

Made in the USA
Columbia, SC
07 May 2024